American History Mysteries

Spellbinding Reproducible Mystery Stories
That Students Read & Solve to Learn About
Important Events in American History

by

Lucinda Landon

SCHOLASTIC
PROFESSIONAL BOOKS

New York • Toronto • London • Auckland • Sydney
Mexico City • New Delhi • Hong Kong

For my parents,
Barbara and Ned Landon,
and our ancestors and descendants

Cover design by Jaime Lucero
Cover art by Naomi Howland
Interior design by Mindy Belter
Interior illustrations by Lucinda Landon

ISBN 0-590-49889-4

Printed in the U.S.A.

Table of Contents

Introduction

In *American History Mysteries*, young detectives Meg and Peter Mackintosh are challenged by a university professor to solve seven history-related mysteries. Intriguing clues to each mystery are entrusted to Gramps, the children's grandfather. During summer vacation, Gramps drives Meg and Peter around the country to the site of each history mystery.

Although Meg, Peter, and Gramps travel around the United States in the order in which the mysteries are presented in the book, the mysteries are independent of one another. The mysteries are arranged chronologically according to their historical backdrop. You and your amateur detectives may tackle the mysteries in any order.

HISTORY MYSTERY 1
Peril at Plimoth

"Plimoth, Massachusetts, should be our first stop, because it's where the Pilgrims landed and it's one of the oldest American landmarks," Peter announced. Peter Mackintosh, his grandfather, were on their way to solve a history mystery.

Gramps checked their list of traveling supplies while Meg and Peter loaded the van.

Lastly, they carefully placed the old chest between their seats in the back of the minivan so that they could study the artifacts and clues as they traveled.

Meg flipped to a new page in her history-mystery detective notebook and started writing.

"We have to answer these questions for each mystery," she showed them to Peter.

"Not necessarily in that

HISTORY MYSTERY 2
The Minuteman's Secret

"Menotomy, Massachusetts, is the next stop on our history-mystery tour," said Peter as he held up the slip of paper. He unrolled a map of the

HISTORY MYSTERY 3
Witness at Washington

"So long Boston! From now on the history-mystery tour is heading west!"

HISTORY MYSTERY 4
The Camouflage Clue in Ohio

Gramps, Meg, and Peter Mackintosh had just solved a history-mystery in Washington, D.C. They were heading northwest towards Ohio, eager to reach their next history-mys-

HISTORY MYSTERY 5
The Warning at Scottsbluff

"Scottsbluff is next stop on the history mystery tour," Peter Mackintosh said as he studied the map.

"What exactly is a bluff?" asked his sister Meg.

"It means to deceive," Peter said with a grin. "For instance, we don't have very far to drive today."

"I think you're bluffing," Meg said as she looked over his shoulder at the map. "We have hundreds of miles to go!"

"You're right," said Gramps from the driver's seat of the van. "And a *bluff* is a high, steep cliff."

"*How much longer?*" Meg teased.

"Why don't you two figure it out," Gramps suggested. "We're in Cleveland. Figure out how long it will take to get to Scottsbluff, if we drive 400 miles a day? We'll go straight on highway—"

"Let's see," said Peter. "The scale of the map is one inch equals 200 miles, and we have to go about six inches."

> **IF THEY HAVE TO TRAVEL ABOUT 400 MILES PER DAY, HOW LONG SHOULD IT TAKE THEM TO REACH SCOTTSBLUFF?**
>
> **?**

HISTORY MYSTERY 6
The Puzzle at Pecos

After spending the night in Wyoming, Meg Mackintosh, her brother, Peter and her grandfather awoke with a decision to make.

"We can continue directly west to San Francisco," said Peter as he studied the map of the western United States. "Or we can go south through Colorado to New Mexico."

"I say New Mexico first," said Meg. "That way we'll finish up our history-mystery tour on the West Coast. It seems appropriate to go from the Atlantic to the Pacific oceans."

"Makes sense to me," Gramps said, so they climbed into their minivan for a jaunt through the Rocky Mountains.

When they crossed into New Mexico, Gramps handed them the first clue for the next mystery, *The Puzzle at Pecos*.

Peter opened the envelope and then sprinkled several small pieces of paper into Meg's hand.

"Professor Brown wasn't kidding when he said Puzzle at Pecos," Peter quipped.

"Quick, let's piece it together," said Meg.

> **CAN YOU DETECT WHAT THE CLUE SAYS?**
>
> **?**

HISTORY MYSTERY 7
The San Francisco Riddle

"San Francisco here we come," said Peter Mackintosh as he gazed at the map.

"How many miles is it from Santa Fe?" Meg asked her brother.

"It's about 1,200 miles," said Peter. "It depends on which way we want to go and where we want to stop. There's so much to see."

"Jot down the places you'd like to visit and we'll make a plan," suggested their grandfather. Meg, Peter, and Gramps were traveling across the country solving history mysteries.

Peter started a list and marked a route on the map.

"While you do that, I'll take a look at my notes," Meg said as she chewed the tip of her pencil. "Hmmm, *The San Francisco Riddle*. I wonder what this mystery is about."

> **CAN YOU MAKE SOME GUESSES ABOUT WHAT THIS MYSTERY MIGHT BE ABOUT?**
>
> **?**

> **WHERE WOULD YOU STOP ALONG THE WAY?**
>
> **?**

The history mystery approach is designed as a way to capture young readers' attention, entertain, and encourage them to think about history and what can be learned from it. Although the mysteries themselves—the artifacts, the children who once possessed them, and the specific events tied to the artifacts—are historical fiction, it is not totally inconceivable that events like them might have happened in the past. The backdrop against which each mystery is set, however, is based on historical fact. Using historical fiction in this way allows students' curiosity about the past to blossom and can lead them to explore history in a more multi-dimensional way. For instance, they may identify strongly with one of the children in the mysteries and want to find out more about the times in which that child lived. In turn students may begin to examine the times in which they live more closely to understand how events are helping to shape their own lives.

Most students love to read and solve mysteries along with the fictional detectives. Solving these history mysteries with Meg and Peter will help them see that historians are very much like detectives. They study clues from the past, pieces of a giant puzzle, and try to fit them together to give an accurate and truthful view of events in our history.

How to Use This Book

The beginning chapter of the book sets up the premise. It explains how Meg, Peter, and Gramps become involved in solving the seven history mysteries and explains the rules of the investigation.

Be sure students have a copy of the **Getting Started** section as they solve the mysteries. They'll need to refer to the illustrations of the artifacts.

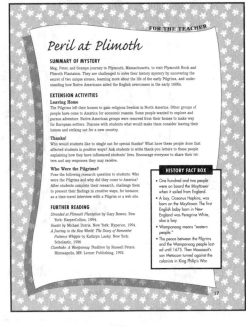

The mysteries themselves are interactive. Students are asked periodically to spot clues and to offer advice. You may want to urge them to keep their own detective notebooks as Meg does.

A **For the Teacher Page** appears with each mystery. This page begins with a summary of the mystery. Three **Extension Activities** follow. These cross-curricular activities provide opportunities for students to read, write, discuss, and research. **Further Reading** lists books related to the historical event that students may enjoy reading comes next. Finally a **History Fact Box** contains relevant facts about the historical context of the mystery. You may want to challenge students to add more facts to a class History Fact Box after they complete the extension activities.

Getting Started

"Listen to this, Meg and Peter," their grandfather read from the newspaper. "On this day in history, June 16th, the following historic events occurred:"

1673	Governor's Island, off Manhattan, bought for 2 axes, some beads and nails
1755	George Washington became the General of the American Army
1845	Texas Congress agreed to annexation by the USA
1858	Abraham Lincoln accepted the presidential nomination
1897	Alaskan gold rush began

"What?" Peter looked up and lifted his headphones from his ears.

"Sorry, Gramps, I was listening to something else."

Gramps sighed, "I was reading about history."

"Oh, you mean ancient times, before television," Peter replied.

"Even before that," Meg rolled her eyes.

"I know what history is," Peter defended himself. "It's memorizing dates and explorers and stuff."

WHAT DOES HISTORY MEAN TO YOU?

?

8

"It's more than that," Gramps explained. "It's learning about real people and how they lived—their beliefs, government, and economy. By studying history we can see how our ancestors handled different situations. Understanding history also helps us to think about how we should handle situations today."

"Think about our old house—all the families who lived here before us," said Meg. "It's pretty amazing."

"Pretty spooky actually. Didn't a Civil War soldier live here?" Peter asked, putting down his magazine. "I think his ghost still lives in the attic."

"He was a Revolutionary War soldier. Remember, we found his grave in the cemetery? I don't know about his ghost."

"Revolutionary War, Civil War what difference does it make?" said Peter.

"There's a big difference," Gramps said, a bit exasperated. "Each event in history teaches us when good decisions were made and the prices humankind has paid for past mistakes," Gramps explained. "And it so happens that something arrived recently from an old friend of mine. I'm hoping that it will inspire you to learn more about history. It's rather curious."

"I love curious things," exclaimed Meg. "What is it?"

"It's in the hall closet," Gramps pointed. "The two of you will have to drag it in here."

Meg and Peter jumped up, raced into the hall and returned, pushing a large old chest.

"It's from the Department of History at the University," Meg read the tag.

"And it's locked," said Peter.

"And I have the key," grinned Gramps.

"And a letter that came with it."

"Well, let's have it, please!" they chimed eagerly.

Gramps handed over the key, and while Meg and Peter struggled with the old lock, he read the letter aloud:

Professor Lafayette Brown

George Mackintosh
Box 222
Foster, RI   02825

Dear George,

     In my travels and studies over the years, I have collected these artifacts of historical significance. They were misplaced from their true home by historical events, accident, or child's play. Many historians have overlooked the importance of children in history as observers and participants of important events. Studying their place in history became a significant part of my research. Knowing that you are a history buff and that your grandchildren, Meg and Peter, love solving mysteries, I thought they would enjoy finding out where the artifacts belong, to whom they belong, and the story behind them. And they'd be helping me out by returning each artifact to its proper home. I have included some clues to get them started on these history mysteries. I think you'll find each case a unique·adventure into America's past

Your friend,

Lafayette Brown

Lafayette Brown

"Wow! I'd really love to solve these cases and return all the arti-facts," said Meg.

"It sounds pretty tricky," said Peter. "Let's see what's in the chest."

"What *is* all this stuff?" Peter asked as he carefully lifted the old artifacts from the chest. "Each one has a label, but they were never filled in."

ABCDEFGHIJKLM
NOPQRSTUVWXYZ
abcdefghijklmnopqrst
uvwxyz 1234567890
Abigail Hopkins April 1775
Age 10 Menotomy
To WD, The secret to the silver
is hidden under the sta

CAN YOU IDENTIFY
ANY OF THESE
OBJECTS?
WRITE YOUR
ANSWERS IN THE
LABELS.

?

doll
compass
sampler
key
lantern
horn
leather pouch

"Here's a stack of paper cards with names on them.
They must be the children in history."
Meg blew off the dust and read:

Xu Ming

Anockus

Joya Gonzales

Eve

Robert Banneker

Abigail Hopkins

Jack Shaw

"Hmmm, interesting names," murmured Meg. "But
how do we know which artifact goes with which child?"

"And where in the United States does each one
belong?" said Peter.

**WHAT ELSE MIGHT
YOU NEED TO
BEGIN SOLVING
THE CASES?**

?

"Is there a map or a list of places to go?" asked Peter.

"Hold on, Peter, there are more papers in the trunk." Meg pulled out seven sealed envelopes. "Each one is labeled with a mystery title and place. These must be Professor Brown's clues to get us started."

The Puzzle at Pecos
Pecos, New Mexico

Witness at Washington
Washington, D.C.

The Camouflage Clue
Ashtabula, Ohio

Ths San Francisco Riddle
San Francisco, California

The Minuteman's Secret
Menotomy, Massachusetts

Peril at Plimoth
Plimoth, Massachusetts

The Warning at Scottsbluff
Scottsbluff, Nebraska

"And look," said Meg, pulling out a large piece of paper. "There's a map."

SCOTTSBLUFF
ASHTABULA
MENOTOMY
PLYMOUTH
WASHINGTON, D. C.
SAN FRANCISCO
PECOS

"The mystery places are all across the United States, from Massachusetts to California!" Meg pointed out. She wrote her thoughts and questions in her notebook.

"Where do we start?" Peter sighed. "What are we supposed to do, mail all the artifacts back?"

"Not exactly," said Gramps.

"I have a little surprise for you that I've already discussed with your mom and dad," Gramps told them. "We're going on a history-mystery tour *and* we're leaving tomorrow in my minivan."

"We're going to visit all these places!" exclaimed Peter.

"With a mystery to solve at each one!" Meg grinned.

"That's right," said Gramps.

"But we don't know which child or object goes with which place!" Peter said, looking baffled.

Meg and Peter stared at the list of names, the map, the objects and the sealed envelopes. "How are we going to figure this out?" Peter asked.

> Where is Menotomy?
> Why is Plimoth spelled with an 'i'?
> Where's Ashtabula?
> Who did the U.S.A. buy Louisiana from?

"We'll have to study each clue carefully, research the historical facts, ask questions, and use our imaginations," declared Meg.

"And see the sights!" exclaimed Peter.

"And you thought this was going to be a boring summer." Meg nudged her brother.

"Why don't I hang on to the envelopes so they don't get lost. I'll give them out to you as we get to each place," Gramps suggested as they repacked the old trunk. "And please try not to bring too much stuff. Maybe one suitcase each?"

"And our detective knapsacks," said Meg.

"And cameras," added Peter.

what to bring:

MAKE A LIST OF WHAT YOU WOULD BRING ON A CROSS-COUNTRY MYSTERY SOLVING TOUR.

?

The Mysteries

Seven Mysteries

Seven places

Seven children

Different faces

Each one has

A story to tell

Solve the clues

Relive their tale

Peril at Plimoth

SUMMARY OF THE MYSTERY

Meg, Peter, and Gramps journey to Plymouth, Massachusetts, to visit Plymouth Rock and Plimoth Plantation. They are challenged to solve their history mystery by uncovering the secret of two unique stones, learning more about the life of the early Pilgrims, and understanding how Native Americans aided the English newcomers in the early 1600s.

EXTENSION ACTIVITIES

Leaving Home

The Pilgrims left their homes to gain religious freedom in North America. Other groups of people have come to America for economic reasons. Some people wanted to explore and pursue adventure. Native American groups were removed from their homes to make way for European settlers. Discuss with students what would make them consider leaving their homes and striking out for a new country.

Thanks!

Who would students like to single out for special thanks? What have these people done that affected students in positive ways? Ask students to write thank-you letters to these people explaining how they have influenced students' lives. Encourage everyone to share their letters and any responses they may receive.

Who Were the Pilgrims?

Pose the following research question to students: Who were the Pilgrims and why did they come to America? After students complete their research, challenge them to present their findings in creative ways, for instance, as a time-travel interview with a Pilgrim or a web site.

FURTHER READING

Stranded at Plimouth Plantation by Gary Bowen. New York: HarperCollins, 1994.

Guests by Michael Dorris. New York: Hyperion, 1994.

A Journey to the New World: The Diary of Remember Patience Whipple by Kathryn Lasky. New York: Scholastic, 1996.

Clambake: A Wampanoag Tradition by Russell Peters. Minneapolis, MN: Lerner Publishing, 1992.

HISTORY FACT BOX

- One hundred and two people were on board the *Mayflower* when it sailed from England.
- A boy, Oceanus Hopkins, was born on the *Mayflower*. The first English baby born in New England was Peregrine White, also a boy.
- Wampanoag means "eastern people."
- The peace between the Pilgrims and the Wampanoag people lasted until 1675. Then Massasoit's son Metacom turned against the colonists in King Philip's War.

Peril at Plimoth

"*P*limoth, Massachusetts,
should be our first stop, because it's
where the Pilgrims landed and it's one of the oldest American historical landmarks," Peter announced. Peter Mackintosh, his grandfather, and his sister Meg
were on their way to solve a history mystery.

Gramps checked their list of traveling supplies
while Meg and Peter loaded the van.

Lastly, they carefully placed the old
chest between their seats in the back of
the minivan so that they could study the
artifacts and clues as they traveled.

Meg flipped to a new page in her
history-mystery detective notebook and
started writing.

"We have to answer these questions for
each mystery," she showed them to Peter.

"Not necessarily in that
order," added Peter. "Do we
know the *when* about Plimoth?
And why do they spell it with an 'i' not 'y'?"

Who?
What?
When?
Where?
Why?
How?

**WHEN WAS
PLIMOTH FOUNDED
BY THE PILGRIMS?**

?

"It's an old fashioned way to spell Plymouth," said Meg. "We know the Pilgrims landed there in 1620, so the mystery must have happened during or after that year." Meg filled in the date.

"Here are the clues from Professor Brown," Gramps said, opening the envelope when they stopped at a traffic light. He gave them the first clue.

Who? Pilgrims?
What?
When? 1620 or later
Where? Plimoth
Why?
How?

-Ä- saved **R**

"Quick, let's read it," said Peter as he anxiously unfolded the old paper.

". . . star saved 'R'? Meg wondered aloud. "What do you think happened?"

"Maybe there was a bad storm, and they were on the *Mayflower*, lost at sea," suggested Peter. "A star could have helped them navigate to a safe place?"

"Maybe," said Meg. "What about the symbol at the beginning of the clue? What do you suppose that means?" Meg copied it in her notebook. "It looks like Egyptian hieroglyphics."

"They might be Native American pictographs," Gramps called from the front seat.

"Hmmm," said Meg. "I think I know which artifact the first mystery is about."

doll
compass
sampler
key
lantern
horn
leather pouch

Joya Gonzales
Eve
Jack Shaw
Xu Ming
Anockus
Robert Banneker
Abigail Hopkins

WHICH ARTIFACT DO YOU THINK IT IS? LOOK AT THE ILLUSTRATIONS TO REFRESH YOUR MEMORY.

?

"I was thinking about this leather pouch. It looks like it could be Native American," Meg said, examining it carefully.

"I'm not sure, but maybe the first history mystery is about the first Americans, a Native American child."

"Maybe, "said Peter, "but the artifact could be the compass. A compass might be helpful if you're lost in a storm."

Meg was carefully holding the leather pouch. "Look, there's something inside," she said excitedly. She took out a folded-up piece of deerskin, which was fragile with age. Something was wrapped inside.

"What is it?" Peter said eagerly.

His sister unwrapped the deerskin to discover two small stones.

DO YOU NOTICE ANYTHING ABOUT THE ROCKS?

?

Meg took out her magnifying glass. "Hey, it looks like there's a picture carved on the rock!"

"It looks like the symbol in the clue. The pouch *must* be the artifact for the Plimoth mystery," Peter concluded.

"It sounds like you're on to something," said Gramps. "Here's another clue from Professor Brown," he said.

"It's a map, show-ing where different Indians lived, "said Peter, opening up the map.

Which Native Americans lived near Plimoth?

"Now we know it has to do with the Wampanoag," said Meg, "since they lived near Plimoth.

"But a rock with a star drawn on it inside a leather pouch. I'm still stumped," said Peter. "How could a rock save someone from a storm?"

"What's so important about two stones?" Meg said, scratching her head.

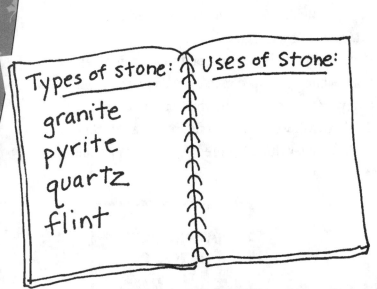

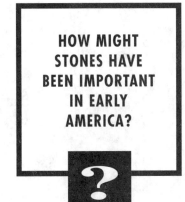

HOW MIGHT STONES HAVE BEEN IMPORTANT IN EARLY AMERICA?

Meg began writing in her notebook. "Here are some possible uses for stones," she said, showing Peter her list. "Since the rock belonged to a child, they might have been used for playing some simple game like marbles."

"Mmm, maybe. They're certainly not shaped like arrowheads."

"Maybe it's a piece of Plimoth Rock," Meg joked.

Uses of Stone:
carving
digging
cutting
hunting
sharpening
building
weapons

"Speaking of Plimoth Rock, here it is," Gramps called from the front seat.

They got out of the minivan and walked over to view the walled in piece of history.

"Well, the two pieces don't look like Plymouth rock at all," said Peter. "It's not as big as I imagined," Peter commented as he got out his instant camera, from his knapsack.

"Apparently it's been moved and broken a few times," Meg read from a guidebook.

"History isn't always what you think," said Gramps. "Come on, Plimoth Plantation is right down the road. They'll have lots of historic information there."

"But how will we be able to figure out a mystery that happened over three hundred years ago?" wondered Peter as he snapped a photo.

HOW WOULD YOU SEARCH FOR CLUES?

?

A few minutes later they arrived at Plimoth Plantation, a re-creation of the original Pilgrim settlement.

"This is a living museum of Plimoth in the 17th century," Gramps explained to them. "The people you see dressed in Pilgrim clothes re-enact life in the village. There is a re-creation of a Wampanoag village nearby. Every detail of daily life is portrayed accurately."

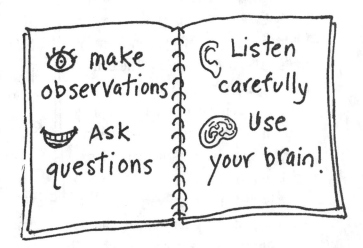

"I really feel like I've stepped back in time," Meg said as they walked through the rustic village and its buildings.

LOOK AT THE PICTURE. IF YOU WERE A CHILD LIVING IN PLIMOTH IN THE 1620s, HOW MIGHT YOUR LIFE BE DIFFERENT FROM THE WAY IT IS TODAY?

?

"The winter months were particularly hard on the Pilgrims," Gramps told them as they stepped into one of the small wooden houses. The ceilings were low and the small rooms dark, lit by only one window. "Many of them didn't survive the first year. They probably weren't prepared for the harsh winters."

planting food
harvesting
fishing
gathering wood
tending animals
hunting for food

spinning yarn
sewing clothes
dipping candles
carving furniture
building houses, barns + fences
(eat + sleep!)

"Were the winters very bad?" Peter asked a Pilgrim woman who was building a fire on the massive hearth.

"Ah yes, fierce storms. It was all we could do to keep the fires burning," she said, speaking in old-fashioned English. Gramps' eyes twinkled. He went back outside.

"Can you imagine spending your whole day looking for dry kindling?" Peter whispered to Meg.

"Peter, that's it! said Meg. "That's what the two stones are for!"

WHAT DO YOU THINK THE STONES WERE FOR? LOOK AT THE PICTURE TO FIGURE IT OUT.

?

"Look how she lights the fire!" Meg exclaimed. "She struck two stones together."

"You're right! The two stones must be must be pieces of flint!" Peter exclaimed, and they ducked out the door.

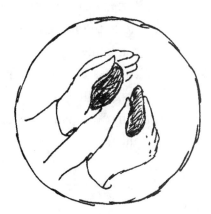

They found Gramps waiting on a bench nearby and told him what they had discovered.

"Good work! And here's some more information for you." He showed them a page in a guidebook. "It's a list of some of the children who participated in the 1621 Thanksgiving feast."

"These names are a little strange," commented Peter. "They'd probably think the same of some of our names today, right Nutmeg?"

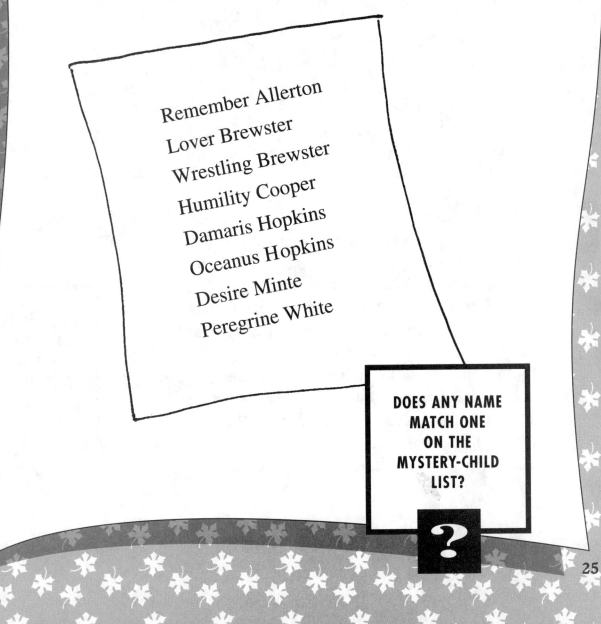

Remember Allerton
Lover Brewster
Wrestling Brewster
Humility Cooper
Damaris Hopkins
Oceanus Hopkins
Desire Minte
Peregrine White

DOES ANY NAME MATCH ONE ON THE MYSTERY-CHILD LIST?

?

"None of the names match the list Professor Brown gave us," said Meg. "But one of the names he gave us is unusual—Anockus—maybe it's a Native American name."

"It's possible," said Peter. "But to find out for sure we should go to the Wampanoag village. Maybe they can decipher this."

At the Wampanoag village, Meg showed the leather pouch to one of the Wampanoag boys. He handled it with great respect.

"This pouch is what we sometimes call a friendship bag, and it is definitely a very old one. You keep important belongings in the pouch." He unfolded the deerskin and gazed at the two stones.

"Are those firestarters?" asked Peter.

"Yes, they're flint. They're important because fire is vital for survival. Then he pointed to the symbol on the rock, smiled, and said, "Anockus—that means star."

"Anockus! That's the mystery child!" exclaimed Meg.

"And the star is the symbol on the rock and the symbol in the clue, too. So the 'R' stands for someone else," Peter reasoned.

"A pilgrim child?" Meg wondered as she stared at the list of names Gramps had given her. "Who do you think it was?"

CAN YOU IMAGINE WHAT THE STORY BEHIND THE MYSTERY MIGHT BE?

?

Meg and Peter thought hard about the pieces of the mystery and began to realize how the clue, the symbols, and the names might fit together. They speculated about what may have happened on a winter night in the 1620s, and then ran to tell Gramps their historical hunch, or hypothesis.

"Anockus must have been a Wampanoag boy who lived near the Pilgrims in Plimoth," Peter concluded.

"He put the symbol of his name on the one of his firestarters," added Meg. "I bet there was a really bad winter storm and many of the Pilgrims were suffering. Maybe Anockus noticed that a fire was out in one of the chimneys, or maybe an English boy or girl came to him for help because they couldn't get the fire started."

"They could have lost their flint or perhaps it was damaged. Or maybe their parents were too ill to help them," Peter conjectured.

"So, Anockus must have given them his stones to start a fire and his leather friendship bag to keep them in. He probably saved their lives. But who do you think the 'R' stood for?" Peter wondered.

"Maybe the 'R' stood for Remember Allerton. We'll never know for sure," said Meg.

"But the leather pouch was never returned to Anockus," said Peter.

"Somehow, Professor Brown acquired it and figured out what the symbols stood for. He wanted it returned to it's original owners—Anockus's people—the Wampanoag."

Meg and Peter took the leather pouch to the curator of Native American artifacts at the museum. She was thrilled to have it for their collection.

Meg and Peter congratulated themselves on solving the case, but they couldn't help imagining what it must have been like to live in Plimoth in the 1620s as a Wampanoag or as an immigrant to the new land.

"I'll never forget the name Anockus," said Meg wistfully.

"Nutmeg, I'll never remember the name 'Remember,'" Peter replied.

The Minuteman's Secret

SUMMARY OF THE MYSTERY

Meg, Peter, and their grandfather visit Arlington, Massachusetts, which was once called Menotomy. Clues lead them to an old house dating back to the early days of the American Revolution. The house sits beside the route taken by a minuteman riding through the area to alert citizens about the threat of approaching British troops. After deciphering a time-worn message, the young detectives uncover the story of the brave young girl who aided the minuteman.

EXTENSION ACTIVITIES

Spread the Word

Ask students to become modern-day Paul Reveres. How would they quickly spread an urgent message throughout the entire community? What form of media and/or transportation would they use? Discuss the advantages and disadvantages of the students' proposals. Then, as a class, decide which method would be the most effective in spreading the word.

Map a Mystery

Pair students for this activity. Have them work together to draw two identical maps of the Boston area—including Charlestown, Cambridge, Lexington, and Concord and natural landmarks such as the Charles River and manmade ones such as Old North Church—as it was in 1775 when the minutemen made their famous midnight rides. Tell one of the partners to trace the route of the minuteman on his or her map. That partner then writes clues about the route. The other partner must use the clues to draw the minutemen's routes on his or her map.

Child's Play

What kinds of games did children play in colonial America? What songs did they sing during the American Revolution? Besides samplers, what types of arts and crafts did children do? Send students to the library to research American games, songs, and arts and crafts of the 1700s. Let them use their research to plan and hold a Revolutionary Days Fair. Invite other classes to join you and see what children did for fun long ago.

FURTHER READING

The Fighting Ground by Avi. New York: HarperCollins, 1984.

My Brother Sam Is Dead by James Lincoln Collier and Christopher Collier. New York: Simon and Schuster, 1984.

Johnny Tremain by Esther Forbes. Boston: Houghton Mifflin, 1992.

The Winter of Red Snow: The Revolutionary War Diary of Abigail Jane Stewart by Kristiana Gregory. New York: Scholastic, 1996.

HISTORY FACT BOX

- Three riders carried the message "The redcoats are coming!" on the night of April 18-19, 1775: Paul Revere, William Dawes, and Dr. Samuel Prescott.
- The redcoats (British soldiers) were marching to Concord, about 20 miles from Boston. They were looking for gun powder and cannonballs that the American colonists were hoarding.
- The British were also looking for the American patriots Sam Adams and John Hancock. The Americans were hiding in Lexington, which is near Concord.
- After reaching Lexington and warning Adams and Hancock, Paul Revere and William Dawes encountered British soldiers. Their horses were confiscated. Dr. Prescott eluded the British and continued on to Concord.
- The first shot in the American Revolution was fired on the morning of April 19 at Lexington.

The Minuteman's Secret

"Menotomy, Massachusetts, is the next stop on our history-mystery tour," said Peter as he held up the slip of paper. He unrolled a map of the United States. "But I can't find any place named Menotomy."

"I've seen the name Menotomy on a few sites near Boston," Gramps told them. "Let's go to a local library and find out where it is, or *was*. Many old villages are swallowed up by bigger towns and lost in history."

Meanwhile Meg was carefully lifting all the artifacts from the old chest and studying them for clues. Suddenly she noticed something that connected the location with an artifact.

ABCDEFGHIJKLM
NOPQRSTUVWXYZ
abcdefghijklmnopqrst
uvwxyz 1234567890
Abigail Hopkins April 1775
Age 10 Menotomy
To WD. The secret to the silver
is hidden under the sta.

WHAT DID MEG NOTICE? WHICH ARTIFACT BELONGS WITH THIS MYSTERY?

?

"What about this old sampler?" Meg suggested.

"What exactly is a sampler?" Peter asked, as he watched for road signs out the window.

"Young girls made them to practice their sewing skills." Meg studied the old cloth. "It's signed Abigail Hopkins. That's one of the names Professor Brown gave us. She was ten years old and she lived in *Menotomy*."

ABCDEFGHIJKLM
NOPQRSTUVWXYZ
abcdefghijklmnopqrst
uvwxyz 1234567890
Abigail Hopkins April 1775
Age 10 Menotomy & to
To WD, The secret to the silver
is hidden under the sta.

"And check out the date!" Meg exclaimed. "Abigail made it in 1775!" Meg couldn't take her eyes off the intricately embroidered alphabet. She ran her fingers along the letters. The colors of the silk thread were faded; the linen brittle with age.

Who? Abigail
What? sampler
When? 1775
Where? Menotomy
Massachusetts
Why?
How?

"Meg, look at the last line she sewed— *To W. D., The secret to the silver is hidden under the sta-'*. It definitely sounds like a clue to the history mystery. Isn't it weird that she didn't finish? What do you think happened to her?"

"We should read the clues before we start jumping to conclusions," suggested Meg.

"Good idea," said Gramps as he handed the envelope to them. Meg opened the envelope. "There's just one clue for this case," she said.

Reflect on this:

MENOTOMY
BECAME
ARLINGTON

HOW COULD YOU MAKE THIS MESSAGE READ FRONTWARDS?

?

"I've got an idea," said Meg climbing into the front seat.

She pulled the passenger visor down and held the message in front of the mirror. "*Reflect* the message in the mirror!"

"Hey! I know Arlington! That's where Willy's cousin lives!" Peter said. "It's by Cambridge, just outside of Boston."

> Reflect on this:
>
> MENOTOMY
> BECAME
> ARLINGTON

"Then we should go to the Arlington Public Library," said Meg as she carefully packed the sampler into her detective knapsack.

When they arrived in Arlington, Gramps went to get lunch, and Meg and Peter headed to the library. "The town of Arlington used to be called Menotomy, the Native American name," explained the librarian as she pored over the old record books. "And yes, there was a girl named Abigail Hopkins who lived here. She was the daughter of Ezekial and Anna Hopkins. She's buried in the old town cemetery up the hill. Her gravestone is probably very worn, but you might be able to find it."

> In memory of
> Abigail Hopkins
> Loving daughter of
> Ezekial and Anna Hopkins
> Born Feb 15, 1765
> Died April 30, 1775
> Sadly taken by fever

"This is creepy," said Peter, "but I like it."

"We'd better hurry," Meg advised. "Gramps told us to meet him at the van at one o'clock. That doesn't give us much time."

After an hour's search, Meg called out, "Peter, I found it! It's so sad; Abigail died of a fever April 30, 1775."

"So that's why she never finished the sampler," said Peter.

Meg took the sampler out of her knapsack. "Look at the last line—I guess Abigail was in the middle of telling someone about the silver when she became ill."

"Yeah, or maybe that last line is just a silly old nursery rhyme," Peter said, taking the sampler from Meg. He stared at the date. "April 1775—I know that date is important . . ."

WHAT HAPPENED IN APRIL 1775?

?

"I've got it!" exclaimed Peter. "It's from the poem I memorized for class, *Paul Revere's Ride* by Henry Wadsworth Longfellow." He recited the beginning, quite dramatically:

Listen, my children, and you shall hear
Of the midnight ride of Paul Revere
On the eighteenth of April, in Seventy-five;
Hardly a man is now alive
Who remembers that famous day and year.

"Peter, you're right," said Meg. "Paul Revere rode north from Boston through this area to warn the colonists at the beginning of the Revolutionary War. He was one of the minutemen! I wonder what his secret was?"

"Quick, let's check with the librarian again and see if he passed through this town. Maybe that's the night Abigail wrote the message." Meg said, dashing with her brother back to the library.

"Yes, indeed, this town was on Paul Revere's route to Lexington and Concord," the librarian explained. She smiled at the young historians before her as she pulled out a map. "William Dawes, the other rider, also rode through Menotomy."

WHAT WOULD YOU DO NEXT?

?

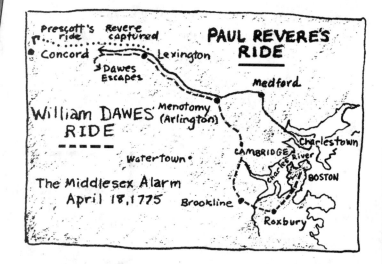

PAUL REVERE'S RIDE

Prescott's ride

Revere captured

Concord — — Lexington

Dawes Escapes

William DAWES RIDE

Menotomy (Arlington)

Medford

Watertown

CAMBRIDGE

Charlestown

Charles River

BOSTON

The Middlesex Alarm April 18, 1775

Brookline

Roxbury

"William Dawes!" Meg exclaimed. She almost fell off the edge of her seat.

WHY DID MEG JUMP AT THE MENTION OF WILLIAM DAWES? WHICH RIDER HAD THE LONGEST ROUTE?

?

W.D.
William Dawes
rode through
Menotomy
April 18, 1775

"The message on the sampler was inscribed to W. D. It's *got* to be William Dawes! Maybe he stopped at Abigail's house to get a drink of water for his horse or something," she said excitedly. "Imagine being awakened by the call, 'The British are coming!'"

"What they called out, Meggers, was 'the *regulars* are coming,'" Peter told her, somewhat smugly.

Meg barely heard Peter; she was so caught up in her thoughts.

"You're letting your imagination run a little wild," Peter cautioned.

"That's what imaginations are for, aren't they?" Meg retorted, turning to ask the librarian where Abigail's house was located. "Was it along William Dawes' route? Is it still there?" The librarian studied another old town map.

"Yes!" answered the amazed librarian. "Abigail's house was on the route, and if it's the house I'm thinking of, it's still standing, though it's fallen into disrepair. It's along the old main road, as many old houses are," she remarked.

"I'm not sure if it's a cape or a colonial design. Let me show you a diagram of an early-American house in this book so you'll know what to look for.

HOW CAN YOU TELL IF A BUILDING IS OLD?

?

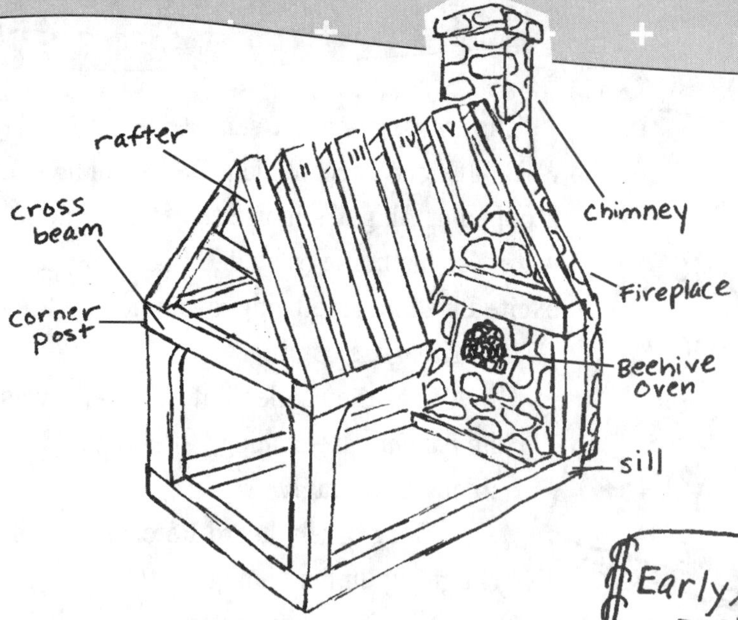

rafter

cross
beam

corner
post

chimney

Fireplace

Beehive
Oven

sill

"Notice how the beams were hand-cut and then numbered and framed together, practically like Lincoln logs," the librarian continued. "Here are some examples of different styles of old houses. Sometimes you can tell an old house by the shape of the roof and other architectural features. You can borrow this book if you like."

"Thanks, we may need it," Meg said, and then she and Peter set off to find the old Hopkins' place. "I'm willing to bet the house will hold another clue to the mystery," Meg said confidently.

Early American Colonial Buildings often have:
- steep roof
- narrow wooden clapboard siding
- Old stone chimneys
- Small windows and window panes
- location close to an old road

WHAT DO YOU THINK IT WOULD BE LIKE TO LIVE IN A COLONIAL HOUSE? DRAW A PICTURE OF HOW YOU WOULD DESIGN YOURS HERE:

?

It wasn't hard to find the ramshackle building, with its steep roof and weathered sides. Some carpenters were there, restoring the structure. They were curious about Meg and Peter's history mystery, so they gave them permission to go inside to search for clues.

Inside, it was dark and the ceilings were low. Doors hung from broken hinges and the wide-plank wood floorboards were slanted with age.

"It even smells old," remarked Meg. "Fortunately, it doesn't look like much has changed over the years." She brought out her notes. *"The secret to the silver is under the sta,"* she read under her breath.

The secret silver is hidden where? | starts with sta:

WHAT WORDS BEGIN WITH 'STA' ?

"It's got to be stable," said Peter. "If Abigail *did* give Dawes' horse water, it makes sense that she hid the silver in the stable." Peter dashed out back to explore, leaving Meg alone in the mysterious old house to think.

She remembered from her history class that many early-American houses had secret hiding places in case of Indian raids, and that often they were found near the chimney or built in under the **s-t-a-i-r-s**!

starts with sta:
stamp
stars
stable
stack
station
stairs

Meg knocked on the wood next to the stairs. One panel sounded hollow. She pulled at it and sure enough, it gave way, revealing a space big enough to hold a small family. Meg got out her flashlight to investigate, just as Peter burst back into the room. "There *isn't* a stable—Meg. . . Meg, where are you?"

"Boo!" Meg yelled, peeking out from the secret door.

"Abigail meant stairs not stable," Meg said. "Come in here and see what's carved in the wood: *'Beehive is the key, A. H.'* What do you think that clue means?"

Beehive is the key A.H.

"We'll never find a beehive," Peter frowned. "It would be long gone."

Meg studied her notes, reviewing all the information they'd learned thus far. "I know what beehive she means!" shouted Meg, playfully shining the flashlight in Peter's face and then running off.

WHERE DID MEG RUN? (HINT: LOOK AT THE ILLUSTRATION OF THE HOUSE ON PAGE 34.)

?

"In colonial times, brick ovens were often made in the shape of beehives. They were built in the back of the fireplace or next to it—just like this one," Meg explained to Peter. Searching the inside of the oven, they found a loose brick, which they carefully dislodged. Tucked behind it was a tightly wrapped piece of cloth. Meg gingerly unfolded the material.

"It's an old key!" said Peter.

"I wonder what it opens? Look there's a letter 'V' on the cloth. Maybe it's a clue."

"I'm stumped," said Meg. She stared at her notes. "We're so close to solving the case. What could the 'V' mean—violin, venison, violets, vase, vault?"

"Maybe the V is upside-down . . . and it means the point of the roof?" suggested Peter.

"Let's check it out," offered Meg, and they climbed the steep narrow stairs to the attic. They searched high and low but could not find another clue or the silver.

Then Meg noticed the symbols carved on the crossbeams: I, II, III. Each symbol on the beam matched a symbol on the rafter it was notched into. She thought about what the librarian had told her about how old houses were put together. "I've solved the mystery, Peter!" she said. "I know where Abigail Hopkins hid the silver on April 18, 1775."

WHAT DID THE 'V' STAND FOR? WHERE IS THE MINUTEMAN'S SECRET SILVER HIDDEN?

?

37

When Meg saw the I, II, and III, she realized that they were Roman numerals and that the 'V' stands for Roman numeral five. She deduced that the silver was hidden near the fifth rafter and the fifth crossbeam. She and Peter found a small tin box wedged into the space there. Meg took the key they'd found in the beehive oven and unlocked the box. Inside was a folded piece of parchment paper with the initials W.D.

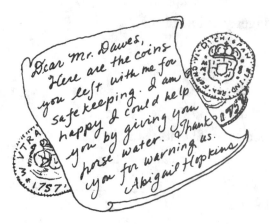

Dear Mr. Dawes,
Here are the coins you left with me for safekeeping. I am happy I could help you by giving you horse water. Thank you for warning us.
Abigail Hopkins

Meg unfolded the parchment and tilted it into the palm of Peter's hand—three silver coins and a tightly rolled note from Abigail spilled out.

Meg and Peter figured that Abigail hid the coins near the fifth rafter and then hid the key to the box in the beehive oven.

She might not have told her parents because she didn't want to worry them, given all the turmoil of the times.

Abigail and her family probably hid in the secret place while they feared the British were marching through town. While in hiding, Abigail left another clue to help Mr. Dawes find the coins, in case anything happened to them. Tragically, Abigail took ill with a fever shortly after that night and sewed the final clue into her sampler before she died. Her parents were probably too grief-stricken to notice the message. William Dawes may have returned for the coins, but seeing a home in mourning, he turned away. Maybe he decided that Abigail deserved the coins for helping him that fateful night.

"But why isn't William Dawes as famous as Paul Revere?" Peter wondered when they told the story to Gramps.

Gramps paused for a second, then said, "Maybe it has something to do with Longfellow's poem about Paul Revere."

"What do you mean?" asked Meg.

"Maybe Paul Revere became even more famous for the midnight ride because Longfellow wrote the poem about him," Gramps went on, "probably because it was easier to find words to rhyme with Revere than with Dawes."

'Listen my children and you shall hear,
of the midnight ride of Paul Revere . . .

"Hmmm," said Peter. "It could have been:

'Listen children and we shall pause,
to hear the story of William Dawes . . .'"

"You'll have to write that poem Peter," said Meg.

"I think I will," said Peter. "'William Dawes, unsung hero.'"

CONTINUE THE POEM ABOUT WILLIAM DAWES.

?

Witness at Washington

SUMMARY OF THE MYSTERY

In Washington, D.C., Gramps passes along some intriguing clues about the development of the nation's capital. Codes are cracked and dark cellars are investigated as the young detectives discover a connection between Benjamin Banneker, who helped survey the capital city, and President George Washington, once a surveyor himself.

EXTENSION ACTIVITIES

Designing the Perfect Community

Talk about the design of your community with students. What do they like about it? What would they change? Then encourage students to discuss designs for a perfect community. List their suggestions on the board. Can students compromise in order to design a perfect community?

A Saying a Day

During his life, Benjamin Banneker wrote several almanacs. So did Benjamin Franklin. Bring in a variety of almanacs and allow students to study them. Then ask students to create their own almanacs. Have them work on their almanacs every day for at least a month. Set aside time for everyone to share their almanac entries with the rest of the class.

Town Time Capsule

Many people had a hand in designing our nation's capital. Who was instrumental in founding, designing, and building your community? Guide students in researching this information. Then suggest that they create a time capsule that records their community's history.

FURTHER READING

Benjamin Banneker by Kevin Conley. New York: Chelsea House Publishers, 1989.

A Capital Capitol City by Suzanne Hilton. New York: Macmillan, 1992.

Dear Benjamin Banneker by Andrea D. Pinkney. New York: Harcourt Brace, 1994.

HISTORY FACT BOX

- Benjamin Banneker was born on November 9, 1731, in the then-British colony of Maryland.

- In 1791 Banneker became an assistant in the survey of the District of Columbia. At this time he also began exchanging letters with then-Secretary of State Thomas Jefferson on the subject of slavery.

- The nation's capital was first located in New York City and then Philadelphia. In 1790 President George Washington selects the site for the new capital.

- Pierre Charles L'Enfant, a Frenchman who fought at Valley Forge, designed Washington D.C.

- A contest was held to find an architect to design the president's house. Thomas Jefferson, using an assumed name, entered the contest. Irishman James Hoban won.

Witness at Washington

"So long Boston! From now on the history-mystery tour is heading west!" Meg Mackintosh called out from the minivan.

"To be more exact, we are going southwest, down the East Coast to Washington, D.C.," said her brother, Peter.

"This is just one of many long traveling days," their grandfather told them. "So I'll let you get started on your next history mystery—*Witness at Washington.*"

"Witness to what?" wondered Meg.

Gramps peered quickly in the envelope. "There are four clues. Here's the first."

Peter looked at the clue. "It's the cover of an old almanac."

"What exactly is an almanac?" Meg asked.

CLUE 1

Benjamin Bannaker's
PENNSYLVANIA, DELAWARE, MARYLAND, AND VIRGINIA
ALMANAC,
FOR THE
YEAR of our LORD 1795;
Being the Third after Leap-Year.

—PRINTED FOR—
And Sold by JOHN FISHER, Stationer,
BALTIMORE

"An almanac is a book of facts that is published every year," Gramps explained to them. "In old days, most people didn't own clocks or calendars, so they relied on an almanac to figure out the best time to plant and harvest crops and fish."

"Well, I know who wrote an almanac—Poor Richard," said Meg as she got out her notebook. "He said things like 'a penny saved is a penny earned'."

"A poor guy named Richard didn't write it," said Peter.

"He didn't?" Meg hated being wrong. She ignored Peter and stared at the old almanac cover. Then she got out her magnifying glass. "Wait a minute. This almanac has clues all over it!"

Benjamin Bannaker's
PENNSYLVANIA, DELAWARE, MARY-
LAND, AND VIRGINIA
ALMANAC,
FOR THE
YEAR of our LORD 1795;
Being the Third after Leap-Year.

BANNAKER.

—PRINTED FOR—
And Sold by JOHN FISHER, Stationer. Co.
BALTIMORE

**WHO WROTE POOR RICHARD'S ALMANAC?
WHAT CLUES DID MEG DETECT?
WHAT DO THE CIRCLED LETTERS SPELL?
WHO DO YOU THINK IS THE NEXT
HISTORY-MYSTERY CHILD?**

?

"Poor Richard's almanac was really written by Benjamin Franklin," said Peter. "Poor Richard was a pen name."

"Oh, right. I forgot," Meg admitted.

"Maybe the mystery is about Benjamin Franklin," Peter suggested.

"No, not Benjamin Franklin," Meg handed him the cover. "The author of this almanac was another Benjamin—Benjamin Banneker. There's a picture of him and his name right at the top."

"So now we know who the next history-mystery child is," said Peter as he glanced at the list. "Ten-to-one it's Robert Banneker."

"He's got to be related to Benjamin Banneker," Meg agreed. "There's more," said Meg. "See the circled letters."

Peter called out the letters, "E-Y-E-P-I-E-C-E."

"Eyepiece?" Meg and Peter were baffled. "What could an eyepiece have to do with the history mystery? Gramps, we need more clues!"

"Okay, here are the second and third clues from the Professor," said Gramps as he handed them into the back seat. "Maybe these will keep you busy until we get to Washington."

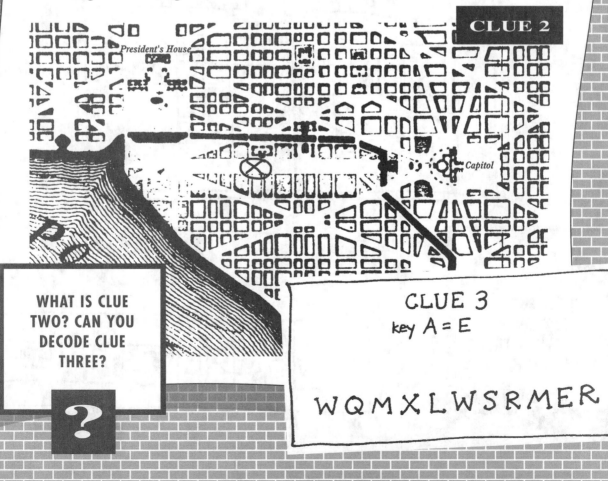

President's House

Capitol

CLUE 2

WHAT IS CLUE TWO? CAN YOU DECODE CLUE THREE?

?

CLUE 3
key A = E

WQMXLWSRMER

Peter stared at clue two. "This has to be an old map of Washington, D.C. It faintly says the 'Capitol' here." He pointed. And the 'X' must mark the spot where we're supposed to go. But everything just looks like a bunch of shapes."

"The City of Washington was designed by a Frenchman, Pierre L'Enfant," Gramps informed them. "He planned the city to be on a geometric grid with diagonal avenues that created rectangles, triangles, and even circles and squares for parks and gardens."

"It's a nice design," Meg said, glancing at the old map. Then she resumed writing in her notebook. "But I'm trying to figure out where we should go first when we arrive in Washington. This is an alphabet code and A=E."

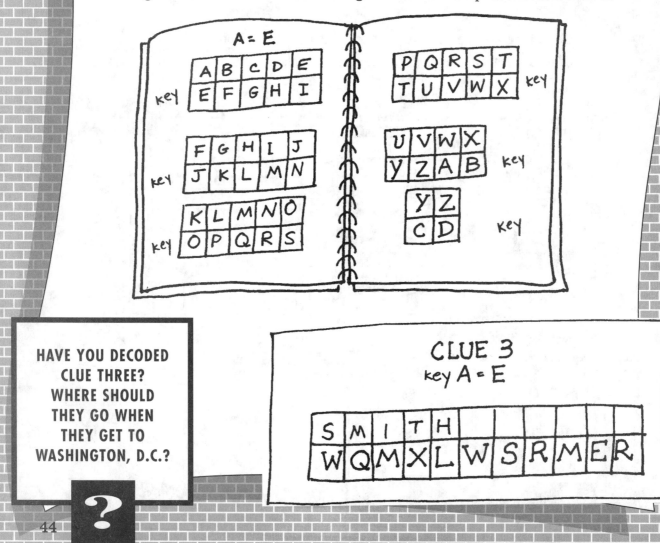

HAVE YOU DECODED CLUE THREE? WHERE SHOULD THEY GO WHEN THEY GET TO WASHINGTON, D.C.?

CLUE 3
key A = E

S	M	I	T	H						
W	Q	M	X	L	W	S	R	M	E	R

"We should go to the Smithsonian Institute!" Meg tossed her pencil in the air.

"That's exactly where I wanted to go," said Gramps. "The largest museum in the United States!"

CLUE 3
key A = E

S	M	I	T	H	S	O	N	I	A	N
W	Q	M	X	L	W	S	R	M	E	R

Peter got out a new city map of Washington to locate the Smithsonian.

"We should go to the Museum of American History at the Smithsonian for the purposes of our investigation," he suggested.

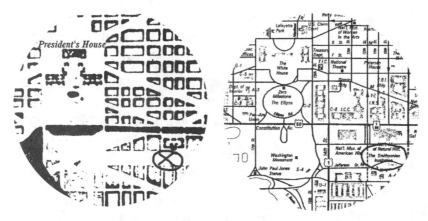

COMPARE THE MAPS. WHAT DO YOU NOTICE ABOUT THE LOCATION OF THE SMITHSONIAN?

?

"Just as I thought, the Smithsonian is located at the spot marked off on the old map," Peter blurted out.

The next morning that's exactly where they went.

Peter bought a history book at the museum bookstore that had information about Benjamin Banneker.

"Listen to this, Meg. Benjamin Banneker was an inventor, astronomer, writer, and mathematician. He was born a free black in the British Colony of Maryland in 1731. Banneker taught himself the principles of mathematics and science and became interested in astronomy in 1788, when his neighbor George Ellicott lent him some astronomical instruments."

"He sounds like he was a genius!" Meg commented as she scribbled down notes.

"There's more," Peter continued. "He was one of the surveyors of Washington, D.C."

WHAT EXACTLY DO SURVEYORS DO? WHAT OTHER FAMOUS AMERICAN WAS A SURVEYOR? WHERE SHOULD THEY GO?

?

"*George Washington* was a surveyor before he became commander-in-chief of the Revolutionary Army," Meg declared. "I read that in a biography about him."

"What do surveyors do?" asked Peter.

"They measure land with instruments and draw pictures of it," said Gramps. "Let's see if this book tells us anything. Oh, here it is. It says Washington chose the site. He met with some of the surveyors. Banneker helped with the surveying."

"Let's see, they started surveying the city in 1791. Wow, if Benjamin Banneker was born in 1731, that means he was sixty years old at the time," Peter figured.

Benjamin
Banneker
1791- survey
-1731- born
60 years old
at time of survey

"That's not so old," Gramps remarked.

"Well, in those days it was. In school I learned the average life expectancy was thirty something," added Meg.

"Maybe this is where Robert fits in," Peter continued. "Maybe Benjamin Banneker brought Robert along to help with the survey. Banneker didn't have any children, but Robert could have been his nephew. He probably had to carry all the equipment!"

"Peter, I think we're getting close to something," said Meg. "Let's ask that guide if there is an exhibit in the museum that will help us."

"There *is* an exhibit of the equipment used when the city was surveyed. Let me show you," said the guide. He took them to the room full of land measuring devices. "Unfortunately," the guide informed them, "a piece of a transit used by Washington is missing."

"I can guess which one," Peter muttered under his breath.

WHICH PIECE IS MISSING?

?

"The eyepiece!" Peter offered, elbowing Meg. "Maybe we can find it," he told the guide.

Meg pointed at another eyepiece in the exhibit. "It would look like this, right?" she asked.

"Yes. But I hardly think you'll find it," the guide said, politely, but doubtfully. "It's been missing for over 200 years."

"We'll see what we can do," said Peter confidently. Then he whispered to Meg, *"Now* what are we supposed to do? We don't even know which artifact is important in this history mystery."

"I was thinking the same thing. Look at your old map, maybe there's another clue. I'll check the artifact list. One of them must have something to do with the missing eyepiece."

"Oops, I almost forgot," Gramps said, looking sheepish. "I forgot to give you the last clue."

Dear Uncle,
    urgent ~ I must
return to the stables.
Go six paces SW
from House of Spirits
to find article.
        Robert

"It's a letter from Robert to his Uncle Benjamin!" exclaimed Meg.

"Is it authentic?" the guide gasped. "This is incredible!"

"What does 'House of Spirits' mean? A funeral parlor?" asked Peter.

"No," said the guide. "In colonial times spirits meant drinks such as ale or wine. House of Spirits is probably a tavern."

"Wait a minute, there is an historic tavern where President Washington stayed while the city was being surveyed," she told them.

"I'll show you where it is on the map."

"Listen to this," Peter said, reading from his book about Benjamin Banneker. "'At one point during the survey, President Washington came to visit the site. He stayed in a tavern and met with other surveyors.' So it is possible that a meeting between the President and Banneker actually took place."

"So Benjamin Banneker might have met with George Washington? Then maybe Robert was there too?" Meg said excitedly.

"Thank you for the information," Peter told the guide. "Don't worry, when we find the eyepiece, we'll give it to the Smithsonian."

WHICH MYSTERY ARTIFACT DO YOU THINK FITS HERE?

?

"The artifact for this mystery has got to be the compass!" Meg said, pulling it out of her knapsack.

"You're right," Peter agreed. "The compass will show us what's six paces southwest of House of Spirits. Let's go."

Gramps hailed a cab and in a few minutes they arrived at the old tavern.

"It's definitely old," observed Meg.

Peter read the compass. "The tavern is facing south," he said.

"Many old buildings were built on a southern exposure to receive the most light and heat from the sun," Gramps informed them.

"What's this stone post for?" asked Peter.

"They would tie their horses to that," Gramps explained.

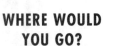

"Look at this old sign with the menu," Meg said. "They certainly had a different way of talking about food. Come, on let's talk to the tavern keeper."

"George Washington did sleep here," the tavern keeper told them proudly. He read the old letter. "But I don't know anything about missing surveying equipment. Maybe the uncle never got the message. Hmmm, you can look down in the old wine cellar if you want. That's where the 'spirits' were kept."

"Sounds mysterious," said Peter. "Let's check it out."

"I'm hungry," Gramps said. "I'll stay up here and sample some fare."

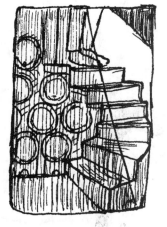

Meg followed Peter down the stone steps into the cool, dark cellar and flicked on her flashlight. "Peter," said Meg. "I don't think we're going in the right direction."

WHERE WOULD YOU GO?

?

"You're right," said Peter. "The needle isn't pointed southwest."

They scurried back upstairs. "Has the sign outside always hung in that position?" Meg asked the tavern keeper.

"Absolutely," he replied. "Every detail in this building is historically correct. That's actually the original sign. Only the paint has been restored."

Meg and Peter went back outside and stood under the tavern sign. Gramps and the tavern keeper followed them, curious to see what they were up to.

Peter read the compass. "Okay, that's southwest," he said, pointing.

Meg took six big paces and ended at the hitching post. "This has got to be it," she declared.

"But where?" They all wondered.

"Robert was waiting out here with the horses. He had to leave urgently for some reason, and he had the eyepiece," Meg reasoned aloud.

"Maybe it started raining," suggested Peter. "So he pulled up a couple of cobblestones and hid the eyepiece underneath them." He knelt down and loosened some of the cobblestones.

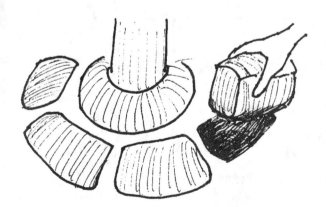

"Go ahead. I'll get a shovel!" said the tavern keeper. "This is incredible!"

Meg and Peter carefully dug beneath the cobblestones until they detected an object.

"It's rotted leather, but there's something inside," said Peter.

Layers of dirt and leather broke away to reveal the remnants of a velvet case that was surprisingly well-preserved. Peter opened it. To their amazement, inside they found an eyepiece and a parchment note.

Master Banneker Please clean this eyepiece this afternoon George Washington

"Is the note from Robert?" asked Meg.

"No . . .," Peter stuttered. "It's from President Washington *to* Robert! It says: 'Master Banneker, Please polish this eyepiece for me this afternoon.' And it's signed 'George Washington.'" They passed the note and eyepiece around in amazement.

"The Smithsonian will be happy to get this eyepiece back," said Meg.

"And a signature of George Washington's too!" Peter said. "Now we know what Robert witnessed in Washington—the President meeting with the surveyors!"

The Camouflage Clue in Ohio

SUMMARY OF THE MYSTERY

While Gramps drives to Ohio, Meg and Peter unscramble a clue and learn about the Underground Railroad. They also discover how Quakers helped in operating the railroad and how the brave exploits of Harriet Tubman guided many people to freedom. An antique doll provides some of the most important clues to this history mystery.

EXTENSION ACTIVITIES

Taking a Risk

As Peter and Meg found out, Harriet Tubman made nineteen trips along the Underground Railroad to lead enslaved African Americans to freedom in the north. Write the word *altruism* on the board, and discuss its meaning with students. What do they think motivated Harriet Tubman to risk her life for others? What might have motivated Quakers to shelter the people escaping from the south?

Passwords to Freedom

The Underground Railroad had "passengers," "conductors," and "stations." Meg and Peter learn that the Quakers used the password "a friend with a friend." Ask students to suppose that they were conductors on the Underground Railroad. Have them think of code words and passwords for different situations they might encounter, such as "danger" or "all clear." Students can write their passwords and definitions in a code book.

Portrait of Harriet Tubman

Who was Harriet Tubman? What prompted her to help others? Tell students to research the life of Harriet Tubman. They can present their findings in the form of a short story, a play, a poem, or a song.

FURTHER READING

Many Thousand Gone: African Americans from Slavery to Freedom by Virginia Hamilton. New York: Knopf, 1993.

Get on Board: The Story of the Underground Railroad by Jim Haskins. New York: Scholastic, 1995.

A Picture of Freedom: The Diary of Clotee, a Slave Girl by Patricia C. McKissack. New York: Scholastic, 1997.

HISTORY FACT BOX

- The first reference in print to the "Underground Railroad" was in 1840.
- Jarmain Wesley Loguen, once a slave, was known as the "Underground Railroad King." He helped over 1,500 fugitives slaves flee into Canada.
- Three different "lines" on the Underground Railroad met at Levi Coffin's house in Indiana. Coffin was sometimes referred to as the "President" of the Underground Railroad.
- Harriet Tubman was born into slavery in 1820 or 1821. In 1849 she escaped to the north. Harriet's first trip as a "conductor" occurred when she helped her sister Mary and her family travel from Baltimore to freedom in Philadelphia.

The Camouflage Clue in Ohio

Gramps, Meg, and Peter Mackintosh had just solved a history-mystery in Washington, D.C. They were heading northwest towards Ohio, eager to reach their next history-mystery destination.

"We need to find somewhere in Ohio called Ashtabula," said Meg as she scanned the map.

"Ashtabula? What kind of a name is that?" asked Peter. "Some of these places have strange sounding names."

"I'm not sure," said Meg. "We'll have to find that out when we get there."

"It will be a while before we get to Ohio," said Gramps as got out the envelope labeled "Camouflage Clue in Ohio." He pulled out a piece of paper and handed it to them. This clue ought to keep you occupied for a while."

"But it's all mixed up!" said Peter. "Professor Brown is full of surprises!"

"Quick, let's unscramble it to get the message," said Meg.

Srocs   a   gimac   inle
Teg   elhp   morf   rifends
Lowolf   het   thorn   rats
Intra   veltra   ot   tomher   H

DECIPHER THE CLUE. WHAT DO YOU THINK IT MEANS?

?

Srocs a gimac inle
cross a magic line

Teg elhp morf rifends
Get help from friends

Lowolf het thorn rats
follow the north star

Intra veltra ot tomher H
train travel to mother H

"Cross a magic line to what? Who are the friends? Follow the North Star on a train? What kind of railroad does that? Who's 'Mother H?'" asked Peter.

"Peter, that's it—railroad! Maybe it means the Underground Railroad," Meg speculated.

"It's possible," Peter agreed. "In school we learned that thousands of slaves escaped from the southern states on the Underground Railroad in the mid 1800s.

"But which artifact and which child?" wondered Meg.

doll
compass
sampler
key
lantern
horn
leather pouch

Joya Gonzales
Eve
Jack Shaw
Xu Ming
Anockus
Robert Banneker
Abigail Hopkins

CAN YOU GUESS WHICH ARTIFACT IS PART OF THIS MYSTERY?

?

"I bet it's the lantern," said Peter. "They probably needed it to find their way in the darkness."

"Maybe," said Meg. "We still don't have much information. And what is The Camouflage Clue?"

"I don't know," answered Peter. "Maybe a clue hidden on something?"

After a while Meg and Peter both dozed off thinking about the clue.

Gramps woke them up when they crossed the Ohio River from West Virginia into Ohio. Then he pulled into a nearby diner to feed his hungry travelers.

"Do you know if Ohio was part of the Underground Railroad?" Meg asked the waitress after she'd taken their order.

"As a matter of fact, this part of Ohio was heavily traveled by escaping slaves on the Underground Railroad because it was so close to the slave state of West Virginia," the waitress told them. "Once the runaways crossed the Ohio River, they were on their way to freedom."

"I forget, why did they call it the Underground Railroad?" Peter asked.

WHY DID THEY CALL THE ESCAPE ROUTE THE UNDERGROUND RAILROAD?

?

"Well," the waitress said, leaning on the counter, "my history teacher told us that the name came from a story about a slave who ran away from Kentucky by swimming across the Ohio River. When his owner searched all over but couldn't find him, he was so bewildered he said that the slave must have escaped on an 'underground road!'"

"The name fits because it was so secretive," Peter added.

"And they called the safe places the slaves traveled to 'stations' and the leaders were called 'conductors'," the waitress continued. "Once the slaves crossed the river and headed upstream, it was harder for the owners to follow the tracks."

There was a map of Ohio on the placemats. Peter traced a route due north from West Virginia to Ashtabula with his finger. "Look, Meg," he said. "If they followed the North Star directly they would arrive in Ashtabula. I wonder what's there?"

"A lot of Quakers helped to hide the escaped slaves," said Gramps.

"There's a Quaker Meeting House not far from here in Mount Pleasant," the waitress told them. "You might want to visit it."

"Maybe the Quakers were the 'friends'—and I think we know what the 'magic line to cross' is," Meg said, and Peter agreed.

WHO WERE THE QUAKERS? WHAT IS THE MAGIC LINE TO CROSS?

?

"Actually the Quakers do call themselves the Society of Friends. They believe in equality of all people and nonviolence," Gramps told them. "They were very much opposed to slavery. I'll take you to that meeting house first thing in the morning."

"And 'crossing the magic line' has to mean 'crossing over into freedom!'" Meg exclaimed. "The Ohio River must be part of the magic line!"

That night they camped out, whispering in the tent about the upcoming mystery and the mystery artifacts. Peter stuck a flashlight in the old lantern. "Imagine carrying this light through the woods in the middle of the night trying to escape. It's pretty scary," he remarked.

Before Meg snuggled into her sleeping bag, she picked up the doll that lay on the bottom of the musty old chest. Meg gazed at her sweet face and wondered whom she might have belonged to. She was made of plain coarse cotton, but her features were carefully sewn in delicate stitches. Her hair was made of black yarn. She wore a red dress with a petticoat underneath.

"Someone loved her a lot," Meg thought to herself. "I wish she could tell us her story. I have a hunch that she's the Ohio mystery artifact. Maybe she traveled on the Underground Railroad."

Meg fell asleep with the doll next to her, wondering what the doll's name might have been and imagining the doll's owner. "She must have been so frightened," thought Meg as she drifted off to sleep with the doll beside her.

WHICH ARTIFACT DO YOU THINK IS INVOLVED IN WITH THE OHIO MYSTERY? WHY?

?

The next morning, they pulled up in front of the Quaker Meeting House.

"It's a beautiful building," remarked Gramps. "So peaceful and plain. The Quakers often worship in silence."

The caretaker invited them inside and explained how the Quakers helped the runaway slaves.

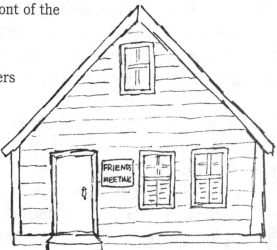

"The password was 'a friend with a friend,'" he whispered. "They hid the slaves in their houses, barns, and businesses. Then they secretly moved them hidden in carriages and wagons from station to station."

Then he showed them a map of sites in Ohio that were possible stops on the Underground Railroad.

"We're on the right track, Meg-O," Peter said, nudging her. "I see a clue in Ashtabula."

DO YOU SEE A CLUE ON THE MAP?

?

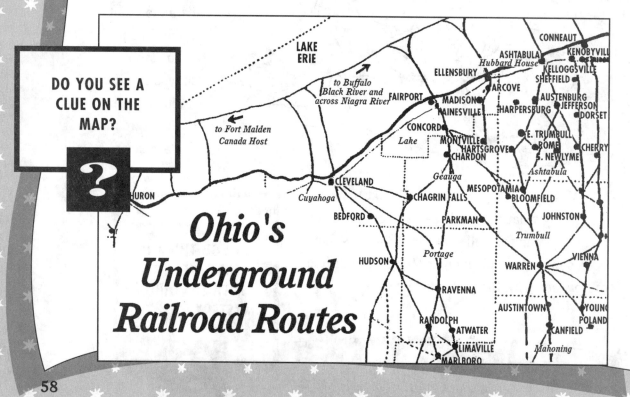

Ohio's Underground Railroad Routes

"Look!" exclaimed Meg, pointing at the map. "In Ashtabula there's a place called Hubbard Homestead. It was a station on the Underground Railroad. Maybe it has something to do with the mystery."

That afternoon they drove along the Ohio River north toward Ashtabula. They had picked up some books on the Underground Railroad at a local bookstore, and Meg was intently reading the stories about the escapes. Many were horrifying and sad, but all were stories of courage and hope that the runaways would make it to freedom.

After a while she just stared out the window and wondered what it must have been like to run through the woods and hide along the banks of a river with little protection or food or shelter.

Peter had been reading about the Underground Railroad too.

"I think I know who 'Mother H' is!" Peter declared, interrupting Meg's thoughts.

"Who?" asked Meg.

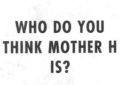

WHO DO YOU THINK MOTHER H IS?

?

59

"'Mother H' means Mother Harriet—Harriet Tubman," said Peter. " She was an escaped slave and one of the greatest conductors of the Underground Railroad."

"It's a good hunch," Meg said. "But didn't Harriet Tubman go by a different code name?"

Peter scanned through his book on Harriet Tubman. "You're right. Harriet Tubman was called 'Moses' because she worked so hard to free her people. She made nineteen dangerous trips back and forth to the South to free slaves."

DO YOU KNOW WHAT HARRIET TUBMAN WAS CALLED?

?

Meg leaned over and grabbed the old doll from the trunk. For the first time, she noticed a primitive scene sewn onto the petticoat.

"Look!" she shouted. "There's a house and a lake, and a river. The building looks like a church without a steeple, and there's a yellow house with two chimneys and some big trees.

Then she felt something hard and lumpy sewn into the hidden pocket on the dress. She carefully pulled apart the tiny stitches.

"It's an old dried up nut of some kind," said Meg as she showed it to Peter and Gramps.

WHAT COULD THESE LATEST CLUES MEAN? TO WHOM DO YOU THINK THE DOLL BELONGED?

?

"Why, it's a walnut. An old shriveled up one, but that's what it is. My neighbor had a walnut tree in his yard. We collected them when we were kids," Gramps told them.

"A walnut from a walnut tree. A house on a lake. Now the pieces of the puzzle are beginning to fit," said Meg. "Let me see that map again." Then she compared the map to the scene sewn on the doll's petticoat. "Maybe this isn't just a pretty design," she said.

"What are you talking about?" asked Peter. "I thought the lantern was the mystery artifact. What's the doll got to do with it?"

Clues sewn onto the old doll: river, houses, trees, lake, boat, star the initial "E" walnut sewn into the pocket

"A lot more than we thought," said Meg.
Just then Gramps pulled up in front of the Hubbard House Museum.

WHAT HAS MEG DEDUCED? WHO IS MOTHER H.? TO WHOM DO YOU THINK THE DOLL BELONGED?

?

"The doll's dress is a map! A *camouflage* map for the Underground Railroad!" Meg exclaimed. "Look! We crossed the Ohio River and then went to a Quaker Meeting house. Our final destination is a house that looks like this on a lake!"

"But what does the walnut mean?" Peter wondered.

"Look at the trees in front and the address," said Gramps. "We're on the corner of Lake and Walnut streets. Walnut trees have probably been around here for a long time."

When they entered the museum, they realized their deductions were correct. The Museum Director told them that the code word for the Hubbard House was '*Mother Hubbard's,*' and it was a destination for many runaways on the Underground Railroad.

"I think our doll has found her home," said Meg. "I think she belongs in a cupboard here at Old Mother Hubbard's. And she had to belong to a girl with the first initial 'E.' See the 'E' embroidered at the edge? The mystery child must be Eve."

"Eve must have been a slave running for freedom. I bet her mother made the doll for her as a camouflage map," added Peter.

"Why don't we call the doll Eve, after her owner," Meg said, giving the old doll a squeeze. "Welcome home, Eve. This is a good place for you to stay and tell your story."

The Warning at Scottsbluff

SUMMARY OF THE MYSTERY

The young detectives and Gramps drive to their next mystery in Nebraska. Here a familiar code piques their interest in early settlers who followed the Oregon Trail. Old tintypes of a pioneer family are among the clues used to unravel a mystery that also involves an antique musical instrument. Along the way, Meg and Peter admire the heroism of another child who lived more than a century ago.

EXTENSION ACTIVITIES

The Best and Worst of the Oregon Trail

Encourage students to discuss what it might have been like to travel west along the Oregon Trail. What might have been the best and the worst things about the trip for them?

Wanted: People with Determination

Let students take on the role of a wagon train boss. Charge them with the task of writing a classified ad urging settlers to travel west with the wagon train. Then have students create an application form for settlers to complete. What kinds of things would it be important for the wagon train boss and the settlers to know? Students can exchange and fill out each other's application forms.

Obstacles on the Oregon Trail

Jack Shaw warned other travelers about the dangers of the Platte River. What other geographical obstacles stood in the way of settlers on the Oregon Trail? Tell students to make physical maps showing the route of the Oregon Trail. Urge them to consider how geography would have affected travelers and to place warning signs on their maps.

FURTHER READING

The Oregon Trail by Leonard E. Fisher. New York: Holiday House, 1990.
Children of the Wild West by Russell Freedman. New York: Clarion Books, 1983.
If You Traveled West in a Covered Wagon by Ellen Levine. New York: Scholastic, 1992.
West to a Land of Plenty: The Diary of Teresa Angelino Viscardi by Jim Murphy. Scholastic, 1998.

HISTORY FACT BOX

- The Oregon Trail was 2,170 miles long. It began along the Missouri River and ended in the Willamette Valley.
- Each traveler was advised to carry at least 200 pounds of flour, 150 pounds of bacon, 20 pounds of sugar, 10 pounds each of salt and coffee.
- It could cost anywhere from $500 to $1000 for a family to outfit itself for the journey. Families had to carry goods and supplies for the six-month long trip plus the things they would need in their new homes—including tools to build the homes.
- White settlers often traded with Native Americans they met on the trail. Settlers would exchange clothing or flour for fresh vegetables or fish.
- Between 1800 and 1900, over half a million settlers got 'Oregon Fever' and made the journey west along the Oregon Trail.

The Warning at Scottsbluff

"Scottsbluff is next stop on the history mystery tour," Peter Mackintosh said as he studied the map.

"What exactly is a bluff?" asked his sister Meg.

"It means to deceive," Peter said with a grin. "For instance, we don't have very far to drive today."

"I think *you're* bluffing," Meg said as she looked over his shoulder at the map. "We have hundreds of miles to go!"

"You're right," said Gramps from the driver's seat of the van. "And a *bluff* is a high, steep cliff."

"How much longer?" Meg teased.

"Why don't you two figure it out," Gramps suggested. "We're in Cleveland. Figure out how long it will take to get to Scottsbluff, Nebraska, if we drive 400 miles a day? We'll go straight on highways."

"Let's see," said Peter. "The scale of the map is one inch equals 200 miles, and we have to go about six inches."

IF THEY HAVE TO TRAVEL ABOUT 400 MILES PER DAY, HOW LONG SHOULD IT TAKE THEM TO REACH SCOTTSBLUFF?

?

Who?
What?
When?
Where?
Why?
How?

"Six inches on the map means about 1,200 miles. If we divide 1,200 miles by 400 miles a day, that gives us three days of travel time," Peter figured.

$$200 \text{ miles per inch}$$
$$\times \quad 6 \text{ inches on map}$$
$$\overline{1200 \text{ miles to go}}$$

$$400\overline{\smash{\big)}1200 \text{ miles to go}} \quad \overset{3 \text{ days driving}}{}$$
miles a day

Meg added up the distances between major cities on the map. "We could stop in Chicago and Omaha and reach Scottsbluff the third day."

"That sounds like a good plan," Gramps agreed. "That will give you plenty of time to read and to write in your journals."

On the third morning, Meg got out her notes on the seven mystery artifacts and children. Then she pestered Gramps to give them a clue for *The Warning at Scottsbluff* mystery. It didn't take him long to give in.

doll
compass
sampler
key
lantern
horn
leather pouch

Joya Gonzales
Eve
Jack Shaw
Xu Ming
Anockus
Robert Banneker
Abigail Hopkins

CLUE 1

· — — · — · — ·   — — — — · —

— · — · · — · · — — — · — —

— · — · · — · — · — — · — — — · —

"What sort of clue is this?" demanded Peter and Meg when they first glanced at the clue. "Hey, it's in Morse code!" they exclaimed together. Meg quickly found her table for Morse code in her detective handbook.

WHAT IS THE MORSE CODE MESSAGE?

?

Morse Code

A ·—	J ·———	S ···
B —···	K —·—	T —
C —·—·	L ·—··	U ··—
D —··	M ——	V ···—
E ·	N —·	W ·——
F ··—·	O ———	X —··—
G ——·	P ·——·	Y —·——
H ····	Q ——·—	Z ——··
I ··	R ·—·	

WAGON

TRIP TO

OREGON

WHAT SORT OF WAGON TRIP ENDED IN OREGON?

?

"The Oregon Trail!" exclaimed Peter.

"You're right," Meg agreed. "The mystery has to be about the Oregon Trail!" She scanned the map. "Scottsbluff is along the way."

"That's got to be it," said Peter. "Hey, once we get to Lincoln, Nebraska, we're practically following in the same path."

"And we're almost to Lincoln," said Gramps. "I'll stop for coffee, and you can have the next clue."

It was a piece of paper, yellow and brittle with age and ripped so they couldn't read all of the words.

May
185
Traged
found u
heavy rai
river swe
carry away Mo
when trying to cr

CLUE 2

WHAT DOES THE WRITING SUGGEST TO YOU? CAN YOU COMPLETE ANY OF THE WORDS OR SENTENCES?

?

"It looks like a page from a diary or journal," suggested Meg. "From what I can make out, it's about traveling on a wagon train."

"It sounds like something tragic happened along the way," Peter said.

"Gramps, do you have another clue? We're stumped."

"Not yet," Gramps shook his head. "We're not even half way there! I've got an idea. Why don't you make a list of what you would bring if you were moving across the country?"

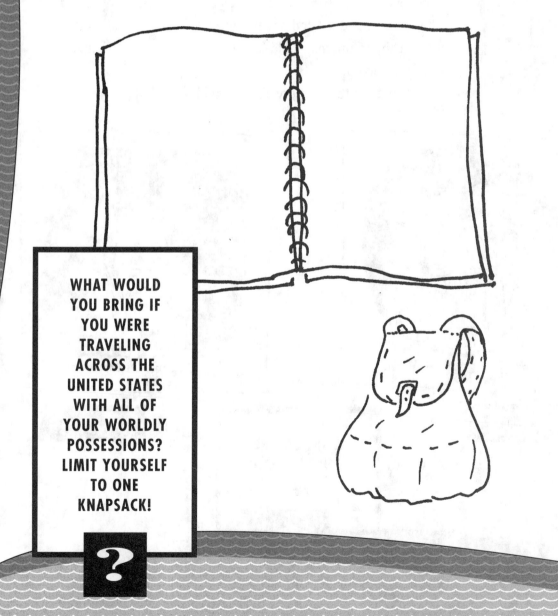

May 185
Traged
found w
heavy rai
river swe
carry away ma
when trying to cr

March or May
1850s
tragedy
?
rain
?
?

WHAT WOULD YOU BRING IF YOU WERE TRAVELING ACROSS THE UNITED STATES WITH ALL OF YOUR WORLDLY POSSESSIONS? LIMIT YOURSELF TO ONE KNAPSACK!

?

NOW TRY TO FIT YOUR FAMILY'S POSSESSIONS INTO THE SIZE OF A COVERED WAGON THAT IS 4' X 12'. DRAW A SKETCH AT RIGHT. (HINT: A COVERED WAGON WAS NOT MUCH BIGGER THAN A MINIVAN.)

?

"Scottsbluff, 50 miles!" Peter said.

"Okay, I guess you're ready for the third and fourth clues," said Gramps, pulling two old photographs out of the envelope labeled *Warning at Scottsbluff.* Then they got back in the minivan and started down the road.

"They're tintypes—old-fashioned photographs on tin," Peter observed.

"I bet it's the mystery child's family," said Meg.

St. Joseph, Missouri 1857

Salem, Oregon 1860

CLUE 3

CLUE 4

WHAT DO THE PHOTOS TELL YOU?

?

Clues in photos
1) 1st taken in 1857 start of trip
2) 2nd taken in 1860 end of trip
3) Six people at start
4) Five people at end
5) Older boy holding horn in 1st photo

?'s about Oregon Trail
1) Total length? ____
2) How long did it take to travel? ____
3) How many miles each day? ____
4) What were the dangers? ____

"One photo was taken when they left from Independence, Missouri, and one when they got to Oregon," concluded Peter. "I wonder which kid is our mystery child?"

"And which is our mystery artifact?"

Meg got out her notebook and looked over the artifacts.

"Peter, look," she said. "One boy is holding a tin horn! It looks like our artifact! That's got to be it!"

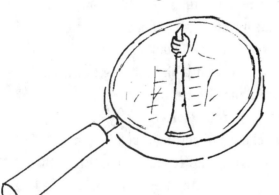

Meg got out the tin horn and continued brainstorming in her notebook, hoping to come up with some ideas about what the warning at Scottsbluff might be. She had some unanswered questions about the Oregon trail too.

Thump, thump, thump . . .

"Uh, oh," said Gramps as he pulled the minivan over. "It sounds like we have a flat tire." They tried to change the tire, but in spite of all their efforts, they still needed help with some rusty bolts.

"Looks like we're walking," said Gramps.

"Walking? How far?" asked Peter.

"Until we get to a service station," Gramps replied. "Come on, it will be good to stretch your legs."

They had gone about a mile when it started to rain.

"This is sort of like what the kids endured on the Oregon Trail," commented Meg.

"Most of them didn't ride in the wagon; they walked the whole way."

"Even in the rain?" wondered Peter.

"Yeah, even in the rain," Meg replied.

As they walked along, Meg and Peter thought about the perils of the Oregon Trail. When they finally got to a service station, they wrote them down while Gramps went with a mechanic to change the tire.

WHAT WERE THE DANGERS ON THE OREGON TRAIL?

?

—DANGERS—
drought thirst
too much rain
flood mud snow
ice fire disease
breakdowns
Indian attacks
wild animals

The service attendant overheard them talking. "Some of my ancestors traveled the Oregon Trail," she told them. "The wagon trains usually had to start out by spring. It took about six months."

"Wow, it took that long to travel," exclaimed Meg.

"If they left too early, they took a chance of getting stuck in a lot of spring showers and mud. But if they left too late, they could get trapped in snowstorms. In fact, there are some real wagon tracks left from the Oregon Trail not far from here. It's stopped raining. Would you like to see them?"

"Wouldn't the rain over the years have washed them away?" asked Meg as she packed up her notes.

"No, the tracks are worn into the rock," the attendant answered. "You'll see."

They followed the attendant's directions to a field not far from the highway they had been driving on. There they found the distinct wheel ruts left from hundreds of wagons.

Peter took a photograph with his instant camera and showed it to his sister.

"Hey, Meg, look how they made signs to warn people of danger."

"Maybe there is a sign or message of some kind on the tin horn," said Meg. She pulled it out of her knapsack along with her magnifying glass."

Meg inspected the horn more closely. "It looks like there are letters scratched into the horn. But it's so faint, it's hard to see what it says."

DO YOU SEE A CLUE ON THE TIN HORN?

The tin horn has the letters

A N E R

scratched on the side.

"A—N—E—R," Peter pointed out. "I bet they're just the letters of the musical notes. He probably etched them on so he knew which finger to play."

"I don't think so," said Meg. "I play the piano, and I know there are no musical notes 'N' or 'R'."

"But, wait a second! It looks like there's a 'G'," said Peter. He was on to something. "That's it! A-N-G-E-R spells anger! The mystery kid was angry about something."

They returned to the service station and waited outside while Gramps paid his bill. They continued pondering over the horn and its inscription.

"I don't know," Meg said, shaking her head. "Anger over what?"

"Look! There's Gramps. Let's get going to Scottsbluff," said Peter.

"Wait a minute." Meg stopped him. "Maybe you were right before about the letters standing for musical notes."

"I'm not sure," said Peter. "But I know where I would take it to find out."

WHERE WOULD YOU TAKE IT?

"Let's take it over to that music shop," said Peter, pointing across the street.

"I bet they could tell us if the letters are notes or not."

"Good idea," said Meg. "I'll tell Gramps we'll be right back."

"This is an old tin horn," the music shop owner told them a few minutes later. "There are letters etched on here, but they're difficult to read. Your sister was right. They're not the musical notes to play. I bet if I rub some of this mineral oil into the impressions, a message might appear."

"The first letter has been practically worn off, but here it's coming up. It's a 'D.'"

"Then it spells 'Danger,'" said Peter, "not anger."

"Why would he write 'Danger' on his horn?" wondered Meg.

"Maybe the horn is from some military battle, and it warned soldiers about attacks from Apaches or something," Peter conjectured. "Or maybe it's from the Civil War."

"There's more," said the owner. "In much smaller letters underneath it says 'crossing the Platte.' And this mark in the middle looks like it was tied to something here because it's slightly bent."

"Excellent detecting," Meg told the owner. She pulled the ripped page from the diary and the tintypes out of her pocket to re-examine them.

"No one is wearing military uniforms in the photos."

"I think I know what the warning at Scottsbluff was," said Peter.

"Me, too," said Meg.

WHAT WAS THE WARNING AT SCOTTSBLUFF?

?

Salem, Oregon
1860

*May
185
Tragedy
found u
heavy rai
river swe
carry away Ma
when trying to cr*

"'Danger crossing the Platte.' The name 'Platte' sounds familiar," said Meg.

"It's the name of the large river the wagon train followed across Nebraska," said Peter. "I saw it on the maps."

"The wagons had to cross the Platte at certain points, and sometimes it was very treacherous," the shop owner told them. "Sometimes wagons overturned or sank, and many people drowned if the currents were rough."

"Drowned? That's awful," said Meg. "And the rest of the family just had to keep going?"

"I'm afraid so," the shop owner continued. "They often left grave markers along the trail."

"Peter, remember the photographs? The whole family wasn't in the second one. I think the mother was missing. Something happened to her along the way," said Meg. "Look at the diary page. I think he's writing about the awful event."

"From the sound of this message written on the horn, I bet that's exactly what happened," said Peter. "I think the horn was left behind as a warning to other settlers that passed that way—to beware crossing the Platte River at that spot."

WHY WAS IT LEFT ON THE TIN HORN? WHAT DO YOU THINK HAPPENED?

?

Peter continued, "He wrote it on his tin horn because he knew it would hold up in all kinds of weather. He probably tied it to a stick and that's how it got indented in the middle. 'Danger'—that was the warning at Scottsbluff."

"There's a faint 'JS' on the inside of the horn," the owner pointed out.

"That must stand for Jack Shaw," said Meg. "That's got to be him in the old tintype—the boy who looks to be about our age. He left the signal to warn other families."

"I think you should take this to the Oregon Trail Museum at Scottsbluff," the owner suggested. "I can tell by the age of this horn and the rest of your information that this is an historically significant artifact."

"That's exactly what we'll do," Meg told him as they both shook her hand and headed out the door.

"First, we have to find our Grandfather and our own *covered wagon*," said Peter.

The Puzzle at Pecos

SUMMARY OF THE MYSTERY

New Mexico is the setting for the puzzle at Pecos. Knowledge of another language as well as the ability to crack codes all have a part in this story. The final solution emphasizes the courage of a young Hispanic girl.

EXTENSION ACTIVITIES

Cultural Contributions

Four different groups of peoples influenced New Mexican culture: Native American, Spanish, Mexican, and American. Discuss with students how different groups can enrich a country's or a region's culture. Which groups have had and continue to have an impact on your community?

Family Artifacts

The Gonzales family's artifacts include a tattered United States flag, a piece of Pueblo pottery, a silver button, and a piece of turquoise. Ask students to think of a family artifact that has been passed down to them or one that they would like to pass on to future generations. Tell students to write descriptions of their artifacts and to tell about the importance of the artifacts to them and their families.

The Battle of Glorietta Pass

Direct students to research the battle of Glorietta Pass. Then have them write chronicles of the battle from Joya Gonzales's perspective.

FURTHER READING

Rio Grande Stories by Carolyn Meyer. New York: Gulliver, 1994.

A History of New Mexico by Calvin G. and Susan A. Roberts. Albuquerque, NM: University of New Mexico Press, 1991.

The Girl Who Chased Away Sorrow: The Diary of Sarah Nita, a Navajo Girl, New Mexico, 1863 by Ann Turner. New York: Scholastic, 1999.

HISTORY FACT BOX

- Pueblo is the Spanish word for 'town.' This is what they called Native American groups they encountered in New Mexico who lived in towns.

- New Mexico was an American territory during the Civil War. Mexico had ceded New Mexico to the United States in 1848 under the Treaty of Guadalupe Hidalgo.

- Settlers from the eastern and southern United States began immigrating to the New Mexico territory in the early 1850s.

- Most New Mexican settlers who had moved from the American south supported the Confederacy during the Civil War. Long-time Hispanic residents and merchants favored the Union.

- New Mexico was admitted as the forty-seventh state in 1912.

The Puzzle at Pecos

After spending the night in Wyoming, Meg Mackintosh, her brother, Peter and her grandfather awoke with a decision to make.

"We can continue directly west to San Francisco," said Peter as he studied the map of the western United States. "Or we can go south through Colorado to New Mexico."

"I say New Mexico first," said Meg. "That way we'll finish up our history-mystery tour on the West Coast. It seems appropriate to go from the Atlantic to the Pacific oceans."

"Makes sense to me," Gramps said, so they climbed into their minivan for a jaunt through the Rocky Mountains.

When they crossed into New Mexico, Gramps handed them the first clue for the next mystery, *The Puzzle at Pecos.*

Peter opened the envelope and then sprinkled several small pieces of paper into Meg's hand.

"Professor Brown wasn't kidding when he said Puzzle at Pecos," Peter quipped.

"Quick, let's piece it together," said Meg.

CAN YOU DETECT WHAT THE CLUE SAYS?

?

meets Palace

Find

artist

capital

silhouette

Go to Where

oldest

Lincoln

Go to oldest capital
Where Lincoln meets Palace
Find silhouette artist

"'Oldest capital'? 'Where Lincoln meets Palace'? Are you sure this clue doesn't belong with Washington, D.C.?" Peter was confused. "What about Pecos? And what exactly are 'silhouettes'?"

"Silhouettes are outlines of objects. The artist might have cut portraits of people out of black paper," Gramps explained.

"Wait a minute," said Meg as she studied the guidebook. "Santa Fe is actually the oldest state capital because it was founded in 1609! That's even before Plymouth was founded!"

"And look on this map of Santa Fe," Peter said. "I think I know where we should go first."

WHERE IN SANTA FE SHOULD THEY GO? PUT AN X ON THE SPOT.

?

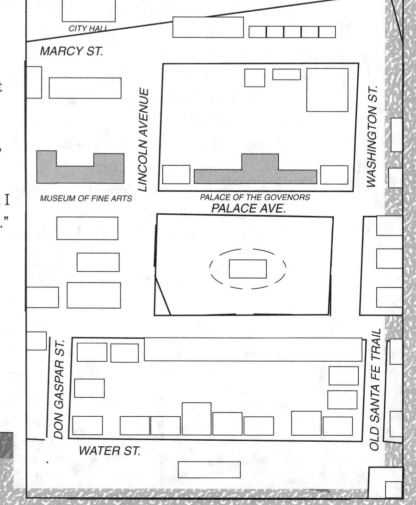

78

"The Palace of the Governors is on Palace Avenue. And there's the corner of Palace and Lincoln streets in the heart of old Santa Fe. That's got to be where we'll find the artist," Peter told them.

"I bet you're right, Peter," Meg agreed and she pulled out her notebook. "Do you have any idea which artifact this story is about and who the history mystery child is?"

doll
compass
sampler
key
lantern
horn
leather pouch

Joya Gonzales
Eve
Jack Shaw
Xu Ming
Anockus
Robert Banneker
Abigail Hopkins

"I don't know," answered Peter. "I just found Pecos on the map. It's about 20 miles southeast of Santa Fe on the Old Santa Fe Trail."

"We still have to find the artist in Santa Fe first," said Meg. "Then we'll take it from there."

Once they had driven into Santa Fe, Gramps parked the minivan, and they walked to the old Plaza downtown. They found the silhouette artist on the corner Professor Brown had directed them to.

"May I do a portrait for you?" the artist asked them.

"Actually, we're here to ask you some questions about a history mystery," said Peter. He showed him the list of seven history-mystery children and artifacts. "Do any of these names or artifacts mean anything historic to you?" he asked.

"Actually, I do recognize a name on your list. What's this all about?"

Silhouette Portraits

R. Gonzales
Artist
Santa Fe
New Mexico

WHICH NAME DO YOU THINK HE RECOGNIZES?

?

Meg stared at the name on the artist's portfolio, then elbowed Peter.

"Joya Gonzales, that's my great-grandmother's name. Why do you have it on that list?" the artist asked, puzzled.

"Mr. Gonzales, we're trying to solve a history mystery that took place in Pecos, New Mexico. Did you ever meet a Professor Brown?" she asked

"I don't recall . . . but I've been working on this corner for twenty years. Perhaps he was one of my customers," he replied. "But some of my family is from Pecos. It's not far from here."

"Show him the artifacts," Meg told Peter.

Peter dug into the knapsack and pulled them out.

"Do these mean anything to you?" he asked.

"I don't recognize the lantern," Mr. Gonzales mumbled as he looked over the artifacts. He juggled the key back and forth between his palms. Meg held her breath. "This could be a key to anything," he said.

Peter asked, "Can you tell us *anything* about your great-grandmother?"

"Not really. But my cousin still lives out at the family home. They operate a dude ranch. Would you like to go for a trail ride out to her place? I'll take you there. I'm done for today anyway."

"Sure!" they agreed.

Mr. Gonzales packed up his easel and artwork.

"I think you're ready for the next clue," said Gramps as he handed it over.

WHAT DOES THE CLUE SAY?

?

cuatro partes de artefactos históricos

"I'm studying Spanish in school," Peter said eagerly. He jotted down his translation on the clue:

"Four more artifacts? What's this all about?" Meg was confused.

On the way to the ranch, Meg and Peter looked up some historic facts about Pecos.

"There's a National Historic Park in Pecos, with lots of interesting exhibits," said Meg and she wrote some facts in her notebook to bring along the trail.

cuatro partes
four   parts
de artefactos
artifacts
históricos
history

Pecos preserves 10,000 years of New Mexican History!

1) The site of an ancient Pueblo Indian Village

2) The Spanish explorer Coronado came here in 1540- and a Spanish Mission was established in the 1600s

3) This territory was under Mexican rule beginning in 1821

4) In 1862 there was an American Civil War battle here and New Mexico became a US state in 1912

WHAT ARE THE FOUR PARTS OF NEW MEXICAN HISTORY IN MEG'S NOTES?

?

Mr. Gonzales knew all the ranch hands who helped them saddle their horses. Then he led Gramps, Meg, and Peter down the trail winding through cacti and piñon trees. It was sunny but not too hot.

"I never knew there were so many colorful plants in the desert," Meg said. She patted her horse. "I could ride all day!"

As they approached his old family home, Mr. Gonazales explained that the buildings and surrounding walls were made of adobe.

Peter trotted up to an old wooden gate, but it was jammed shut. Then they heard someone call out. It was Mr. Gonzales' cousin. She was surprised but pleased to greet visitors as she led them through the more modern gate.

"This is my cousin Lucia," Mr. Gonzales said, introducing them. "These are my new friends. They are detectives trying to solve a historical mystery. It might have something to do with great-grandmother."

"How fascinating." Lucia's eyes lit up. "I do have some things of great-grandmothers I can show you." She disappeared through a dark oak door and returned a few minutes later with a small ornate box. It was made of carved wood with gilt designs along the edges.

"It looks like a miniature treasure chest," whispered Peter.

"My mother told me this was a little collection of things great-grandmother found around the ranch. They're really nothing of importance, but I hate to throw them out." She lifted out the objects. There were three items wrapped in a piece of red-and-white-striped cloth.

CAN YOU IDENTIFY ANY OF THE OBJECTS?

?

Mexican figure

Pueblo pottery

Spanish button

"Just an old button, a piece of turquoise, and a broken piece of pottery," said Peter.

"These aren't just broken old pieces," exclaimed Mr. Gonzales. "This is an ancient piece of Pueblo pottery! And this silver button has Spanish on it."

"Wow!" said Peter. "Those are really old. What about this piece of turquoise?"

"That looks like a Mexican design," added Lucia.

"So each artifact is from a different group of people who lived here!" suggested Peter. "I think your great-grandmother was some kind of history buff!"

"Or archeologist," added Meg as she looked over her research notes on Pecos. "Too bad there isn't anything from the American Civil War. There was a battle near here."

"That's right," said Lucia. "I remember my father telling me that Union soldiers hid at the ranch."

"Meg, *'cuatro partes de artefactos históricos'* . . . four artifacts of history!" Peter exclaimed.

"But there are only three," said Meg. "One's missing!"

"Think again!" said Peter. "There are four artifacts of history here! Look at this piece of red-and-white striped cloth."

"So? It looks like an old tablecloth circa 1950," Meg quipped.

WHAT IS THE FOURTH ARTIFACT?

?

"Ten-to-one it's a piece of a United States flag! It was probably torn in battle when the Union soldiers were here," said Peter.

"I think you're on to something, Peter," said Gramps as he studied the remnant. "When was the battle?"

"The Battle of Glorietta Pass was in 1862," Meg read from her notes.

"Great-grandmother Joya was born about 1850," said Lucia. "She would have been about twelve. Our ancestors built this ranch like a fortress. Remember that old South Gate in the walled courtyard around the stables? It has been jammed shut for as long as anyone can remember. Father said Joya let the soldiers in through that gate at the last minute before the Confederates arrived and locked it in the nick of time. But then the key was lost. We've kept that gate shut all these years."

"Your old key," said Mr. Gonzales. "It could be for a gate like this."

Meg fumbled in her knapsack and pulled out the old key. "Let's try it!"

They hurried to the ancient adobe wall. Lucia fit the key into the old lock and twisted it. The old lock clunked open, but the door wouldn't budge. They pushed so hard that the lock casing fell down in between the boards of the hollow door.

Peter stuck his hand inside the gap to retrieve the pieces. "There's something inside here." As he pulled, one panel of wood fell away. Hidden inside the hollow door was a rolled-up piece of cloth. It was red-and-white striped with blue stars. Where one corner had been ripped, Joya's piece fit in.

"It's the American flag!" exclaimed Peter. "The soldiers must have hid it here during the battle. Do you think the flag had been jamming the lock all these years?"

"Maybe they left it here for Joya in thanks for saving them!" said Lucia.

"Now there are cinquo artefactos for your family collection, including the key," said Meg. "Another history mystery solved."

"Amazing," said Mr. Gonzales. "Allow me to cut your silhouettes in thanks." And they did.

The San Francisco Riddle

SUMMARY OF THE MYSTERY

A visit to Chinatown gets Meg and Peter involved in a mystery that includes Chinese symbols, a cryptic poem, and a pair of antique lanterns. The detective team uncovers a valuable Chinese artifact and learns lessons about how railroads brought east and west together, how immigrants contributed to the nation's growth, and how two brave brothers helped each other in times of trouble.

EXTENSION ACTIVITIES

Planes and Trains

Display a map of the United States. Remind students that before the transcontinental railroad was completed in 1869, people had to travel from coast to coast by ship, sailing around South America, or by stagecoach, wagon, or horseback. Discuss how transportation has changed since then. How do they think the joining of the nation by railroad changed our country? Ask them how they think transportation will change in the future.

Strike It Rich

Encourage students to imagine that they joined the gold rush to California. Ask them to choose the number 1 or 2. Explain that 1 means they struck it rich and 2 means they busted. Tell students to write letters home describing their successes or failures.

Working on the Railroad

Chinese and Irish immigrants played an important role in the building of the transcontinental railroad. Have students research the building of the Union Pacific railroad from the east and the Central Pacific railroad from the west. What were working conditions like for laborers? What kinds of jobs did they have?

FURTHER READING

The Journal of Sean Sullivan by William Durbin. New York: Scholastic, 1999.

The Ten Mile Day by Mary Ann Fraser. New York: Henry Holt, 1993.

Tales from Gold Mountain by Paul Yee. Toronto: Groundwood Books, 1999.

HISTORY FACT BOX

- Chinese railroad workers were paid $1 day. The Central Pacific sent ships to China to bring 7,000 Chinese workers to the United States.

- Workers on the Union Pacific were mostly ex-Confederate soldiers, formerly enslaved men, and Irish immigrants.

- On May 10, 1869, a golden spike was driven into the rails joining the Central Pacific and the Union Pacific Railroads. Leland Stanford, president of the Central Pacific, missed the spike on his first try. Later Chinese workers were ordered to replace the gold spike with a regular spike.

The San Francisco Riddle

Map labels:
5 · 80 · UTAH · Colorado River · South Platte River · Denver · 15 · 70 · 25 · Sacramento · CALIFORNIA · NEVADA · BRYCE CANYON · 80 · 580 · San Francisco · YOSEMITE NATIONAL PARK · ZION NATIONAL PARK · COLORADO · MONTEREY BAY NATIONAL MARINE SANCTUARY · DEATH VALLEY · GRAND CANYON · Santa Fe · Pecos · 5 · SEQUOIA NATIONAL PARK · SUNSET CRATER VOLCANO · HOOVER DAM · 40 · Flagstaff · 40 · 101 · HOLLYWOOD · 40 · 17 · 10 · Phoenix · 25 · CARLSBAD CAVERNS · Los Angeles · 10 · CASA GRANDE RUINS · 8 · NEW MEXICO · San Diego · 10 · ARIZONA

"San Francisco here we come," said Peter Mackintosh as he gazed at the map.

"How many miles is it from Santa Fe?" Meg asked her brother.

"It's about 1,200 miles," said Peter. "It depends on which way we want to go and where we want to stop. There's so much to see."

"Jot down the places you'd like to visit and we'll make a plan," suggested their grandfather. Meg, Peter, and Gramps were traveling across the country solving history mysteries.

Peter started a list and marked a route on the map.

"While you do that, I'll take a look at my notes," Meg said as she chewed the tip of her pencil. "Hmmm, *The San Francisco Riddle.* I wonder what this mystery is about."

WHERE WOULD YOU STOP ALONG THE WAY?

?

CAN YOU MAKE SOME GUESSES ABOUT WHAT THIS MYSTERY MIGHT BE ABOUT?

?

Meg thought about the artifacts. "This lantern is interesting," said Meg as she examined it with her magnifying glass. "It's made of a metal, and oil must have been poured in the base and then burned with this withered wick," she observed.

"What kind of a design is that?" She showed it to Peter.

"Clean it off and we'll have a better idea." He tossed her a paper towel.

Meg rubbed the lantern softly. "Maybe a genie will appear, and I'll be granted three wishes!" she joked.

"Let's wish that Gramps will stop in all of the places on my list," said Peter.

"Look!" said Meg. "I think it's a Chinese character. Xu Ming sounds Chinese. I think we know who the history-mystery child is!"

"And the Chinese character might be a clue to our destination once we're in San Francisco," said Peter as he showed Meg a map of the city.

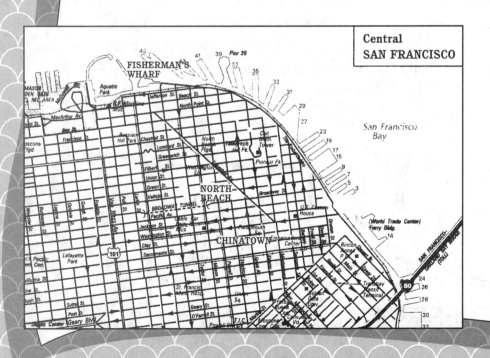

WHERE WOULD YOU GO IN SAN FRANCISCO?

"Chinatown!" exclaimed Meg. "I can hardly wait!"

"There are lots of exciting places to see on our way," said Gramps. "We'll try to cover as much of Peter's list as we can."

Gramps was right. All of the National Parks were exciting. But a few days later, when they headed into the city limits of San Francisco, Meg and Peter were happy to return to their investigation.

"Here's the clue from the professor," said Gramps.

> *Look within to be told*
> *About my twin and the hidden gold.*
> *Far-away brother lost the strike,*
> *City brother saved the spike.*

WHAT DO YOU THINK THE RIDDLE MEANS? WHERE WOULD YOU LOOK?

?

"It's a riddle," Meg said, puzzling over the clue. "The twin has the gold. Maybe Xu Ming had a twin brother?"

"Where do we start?" asked Peter.

"We start by parking the minivan and taking a trolley," said Gramps. "Driving up and down these hills is exasperating!"

Who?
What?
When?
Where?
Why?
How?

While Gramps found a place to park, Peter opened his history book to do some research on Chinese immigration to America. Meg continued to puzzle over the riddle.

WHEN DID THE CHINESE START COMING TO AMERICA? WHY DID THEY COME?

?

"Maybe the lantern has something to do with the gold rush," suggested Meg.

"Or building the railroads," said Peter. "It could have been used to light tunnels they were digging."

"Or gold mines?" said Meg.

"Or both," said Gramps. "Many Chinese came to California to look for gold, like everyone else did. Some left their families behind in China with plans to return with their fortune. But when the gold rush ended, they stayed on to help build the railroads."

Who? Xu Ming
What? lantern
When? 1850's
Where? San Francisco
Why? To work on railroads
To find GOLD
How? The Chinese crossed the Pacific Ocean in boats

Meg thought hard, then reread the clue. "'Look within to be told.' There's got to be a clue inside this lantern somewhere," she said. She undid the stopper that had once held in the oil, but couldn't detect anything inside.

"Wait a minute," she mumbled, turning the lantern over. "These tin columns seem hollow." Sure enough, she was able to undo a circle of tin on the base that opened up to a hollow shaft. Inside was a rolled-up piece of paper.

"It looks like a Chinese scroll," said Peter, amazed.

Meg unrolled the thin paper, but she couldn't read the message. "It's in Chinese."

月月、两兄弟交换了灯笼

"Come on," Peter said, practically pushing her out the door of the minivan. "Let's go to Chinatown and find someone to translate."

DO YOU NOTICE ANYTHING ABOUT THE SYMBOLS?

?

"It says, 'Ming Brothers switch lanterns,'" the conductor told them. They thanked him as they spun off the trolley in Chinatown.

"That's the same symbol that's on the lantern. This lantern obviously belonged to the Ming family!" Peter asserted.

"What was the brother safe from?" wondered Meg.

"I'm still trying to figure out what 'strike' and 'spike' have to do with the mystery," said Peter, scratching his head.

Peter found a phone booth and pulled out the local directory. "Gee, there are so many Mings."

"Peter, this is hopeless," said Meg as she gazed over his shoulder. "Let's try a different tactic."

"Not so fast, Meg-o. Look at this listing," said Peter.

WHAT DID PETER NOTICE?

Ming, W. Far Away Antiques

"'W. Ming Far-Away Antiques!' Do you suppose there's a connection?" asked Peter, jotting down the address.

"It's in Chinatown. It can't be too far away," Meg answered him and they set off in search of the antique shop.

A few minutes later, they found it. A bell gently rang as they pushed open the door and entered the store.

Meg gazed around the dimly lit room. "So much neat stuff."

Gramps pointed to some pictures on the wall. "Here are some very old photographs of men working on the railroad."

"Conditions don't look very good," said Meg. "They worked all winter, even in the snow?"

"That's true," said a young man behind the counter. "The working conditions were deplorable, and the Chinese men who built the railroad worked fourteen-hour days and were only paid $28 a month."

"I read about that," said Peter. "The Central Pacific Railroad was in a hurry to connect with the Union Pacific Railroad to become the first transcontinental railway."

"So they worked all winter to complete the job. They went on strike for better wages, but the owners cut off their food supply until they began work again."

"That's awful," said Meg.

"Strike?!" cried Peter. "Let's see that clue again."

Meg pulled the clue out of her knapsack and the lantern too. She read the end of the clue aloud: "'Far-away brother lost the strike, city brother saved the spike.'"

"Could I please see your lantern?" asked the young man.

WHAT DID HE NOTICE?

?

91

Meg handed over the lantern. Then something on the shelf caught her eye. "Look! It's a lantern like ours!"

"Exactly what I noticed," said the young man as he took down the second lantern.

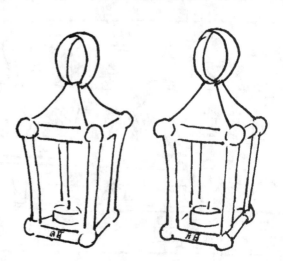

"They're twins," confirmed Peter. "They both have the same mark."

"Where did you find this?" asked the young man.

"It's a long story, but we have been searching for a twin," said Meg. "I thought we were looking for a twin brother, but we found a twin lantern!"

Peter briefly explained about Professor Brown's history mysteries, and Meg showed the young man the riddle and the clue that was hidden inside the lantern.

"Professor Brown must have known that you had the matching lantern," said Gramps. "It's lucky it wasn't sold."

"It's not for sale," said the young man. "It has a special meaning to my family. My name is Wesley Ming. This is my family's store. The lantern is a reminder of the hard work my ancestors did when they came to this country. And you *were* looking for a pair of twin brothers, my great-great uncles. You were looking at their photograph a moment ago, Xu Ming and Kam Ming."

"The twin brothers had twin lanterns!" said Peter as he held them up. "That's odd, your lantern is much heavier. I mean a lot heavier." He handed the lanterns to Wesley to judge.

"You're right. Even though they seem to be identical," said Wesley.

"Peter, that's it!" said Meg. "You just solved this history mystery!"

WHAT IS MEG GETTING AT?

?

"I bet there's something hidden inside of your lantern too," said Meg. "I'll show you." She carefully turned the lantern over and removed the piece on the bottom like she had before. A heavy, shiny object slid out.

"What is it?" asked Gramps.

"It's gold!" exclaimed Peter. "No wonder it was so heavy!"

"It looks like a gold spike. Like the spikes they drove into the railroad ties," said Wesley. "And there's a piece of paper with a message." He translated, "'Brothers switch places.' I can't believe this has been found! It's from my twin uncles!"

"That's like the message we had, only ours said 'Brothers switch lanterns,'" explained Peter.

"They switched lanterns and places? What's this all about?" asked Meg.

"The story is that Kam Ming went to work on the railroad and Xu stayed behind in San Francisco," said Wesley. "When Xu heard about the strike, he sneaked into the camp to make sure his brother was okay, carrying the lantern to find his way. Maybe he brought food and clothing. When he found his brother in poor health, Xu switched places with Kam and sent him back to San Francisco—they were identical twins, so no one noticed."

"But why did they switch lanterns too?" Peter asked.

"The lanterns held the messages. The old family must have known about the secret hiding places. If something happened to either of them, the message would explain. A Chinese worker always would return the lantern to the Ming family," said Wesley.

"Kam, the twin on the railroad brought the golden spike back with him," he concluded. "Chinese workers often made precious things out of the gold they had mined and hid the items to get them back to China."

"A narrow spike fit into the hollow hiding place," said Meg.

"It's also like the golden spike that they drove in when they connected the two railroads at Promontory Point!" added Peter.

"Only this spike commemorates the Chinese workers!" said Wesley proudly. "These are small signatures of workers on the spike—my ancestors and their friends! I'm so glad you found me. I never would have known the spike was hidden in here."

"Now the twin lanterns have found each other," said Meg.

"They make a nice pair," added Peter.

"So near and yet so far away," mused Gramps, as he gave Meg and Peter a hug. "Case closed."

About the Author

Author and illustrator Lucinda Landon was born on August 15, 1950, in Galesburg, Illinois. Her family moved to Schenectady, New York, where she and her three sisters grew up. She comes to children's books with a background in art and design, having attended the Sir John Cass School of Art in London, St. Lawrence University, and the Rhode Island School of Design. She has worked as an art museum guide, children's librarian, and special education teacher.

The first book she illustrated, *The Young Detective's Handbook* by William Vivian Butler, received a special Edgar Allan Poe Award from the Mystery Writers of America in 1981. A character from that handbook evolved into Meg Mackintosh. Meg was also inspired by a childhood friend named Meg, but Landon admits that Meg Mackintosh is also a bit like her.

Landon has always loved reading mysteries and remembers that there weren't many for middle readers when she was growing up, especially with girl detectives and clues in the pictures.

"Writing the Meg Mackintosh series," says Landon, "gives me the opportunity to combine my love of drawing and mysteries. It's fun to design books with the clues hidden in both the text and the black-and-white illustrations." Landon says she likes to keep her mysteries fast paced, with intriguing clues and questions posed to the reader to see if they can match wits with Meg.

Lucinda Landon is married to photographer Jim Egan and has two sons, Alexander and Eric, two dogs, two cats and a horse named Olive. They live in an old house in Rhode Island that was built in 1709. The house has a hidden trap door to the basement and a secret hiding place behind the chimney. "It's a great place to write mysteries," says Landon.

Other books in the Meg Mackintosh series published by Secret Passage Press include :

Meg Mackintosh and the Case of the Curious Whale Watch
Meg Mackintosh and the Mystery at the Medieval Castle
Meg Mackintosh and the Mystery at Camp Creepy
Meg Mackintosh and the Mystery in the Locked Library

Vist Meg and Peter at megmackintosh.com!